The FRIEND® Program
for Creating Supportive Peer Networks for Students with Social Challenges, including Autism

of related interest

Flying Starts for Unique Children
Top Tips for Supporting Children with SEN or Autism When They Start School
Adele Devine
ISBN 978 1 78592 001 1
eISBN 978 1 78450 241 6

Autism Spectrum Disorder and the Transition into Secondary School
A Handbook for Implementing Strategies in the Mainstream School Setting
Marianna Murin, Josselyn Hellriegel and Will Mandy
ISBN 978 1 78592 018 9
eISBN 978 1 78450 262 1

The Green Zone Conversation Book
Finding Common Ground in Conversation for Children on the Autism Spectrum
Joel Shaul
ISBN 978 1 84905 759 2
eISBN 978 0 85700 946 3

A Practical Guide for Teachers of Students with an Autism Spectrum Disorder in Secondary Education
Debra Costley, Elaine Keane, Trevor Clark and Kathie Lane
ISBN 978 1 84905 310 5
eISBN 978 0 85700 646 2

Speak, Move, Play and Learn with Children on the Autism Spectrum
Activities to Boost Communication Skills, Sensory Integration and Coordination Using Simple Ideas from Speech and Language Pathology and Occupational Therapy
Lois Jean Brady, America X Gonzalez, Maciej Zawdzki and Corinda Presley
ISBN 978 1 84905 872 8
eISBN 978 0 85700 531 1

Fuzzy Buzzy Groups for Children with Developmental and Sensory Processing Difficulties
A Step-by-Step Resource
Fiona Brownlee and Lindsay Munro
Illustrated by Aisling Nolan
ISBN 978 1 84310 966 2
eISBN 978 0 85700 194 8

What is Friendship?
Games and Activities to Help Children to Understand Friendship
Pamela Day
ISBN 978 1 84905 048 7
eISBN 978 0 85700 198 6

The FRIEND® Program
for Creating Supportive Peer Networks for Students with Social Challenges, including Autism

SHARMAN OBER-REYNOLDS,
CHRISTOPHER J. SMITH and LORI VINCENT,
with HOLLY SOKOL and SHERI S. DOLLIN

Jessica Kingsley *Publishers*
London and Philadelphia

First published in 2020
by Jessica Kingsley Publishers
73 Collier Street
London N1 9BE, UK
and
400 Market Street, Suite 400
Philadelphia, PA 19106, USA

www.jkp.com

Library of Congress Cataloging in Publication Data
A CIP catalog record for this book is available from the Library of Congress

British Library Cataloguing in Publication Data
A CIP catalogue record for this book is available from the British Library

ISBN 978 1 78592 627 3
eISBN 978 1 78592 628 0

Printed and bound in the United States

The accompanying PDF can be downloaded from www.jkp.com/voucher using the code NEYSOJY.

Certified Chain of Custody
SUSTAINABLE   Promoting Sustainable Forestry
FORESTRY
INITIATIVE   www.sfiprogram.org
              SFI-01268

SFI label applies to the text stock

Contents

Acknowledgements

Jessica Sheridan, MEd,
Southwest Autism Research & Resource Center, Phoenix, Arizona

Kathryn Severson, MS, CCC-SLP,
Southwest Autism Research & Resource Center, Phoenix, Arizona

Daniel Openden, PhD, BCBA-D,
Southwest Autism Research & Resource Center, Phoenix, Arizona

Linda Kraynack, MSEd,
Scottsdale School District

Doreen Muir, BA,
Scottsdale School District

Special Thanks:

Karen Donmoyer, Parent

Nick Noonan, Principal

Preface

Our son has autism. We hoped that he would go to school and make friends, but the other kids just left him alone. Andrew didn't have a clue about how to approach and engage with his peers. At recess, he walked the perimeter of the playground and ate lunch alone every day. How did the other kids know what to do? They learned skills so easily, just by observing others. However, it was quite obvious that just being placed with typical peers did not mean that my son with autism would learn what to do so easily. We wanted to help him, but we needed help ourselves. We consulted with Drs Robert and Lynn Koegel at the University of California at Santa Barbara (UCSB), now at Stanford University, and it was their guidance and encouragement that inspired the peer support program that became the Fostering Relationships in Early Network Development (FRIEND®) Program.

Andrew's school never offered a social skills program, so our approach was brand new. We had a lot to learn. Support from Cindy Carter Barnes and Danny Openden, two UCSB graduate students, kept us on track. One of our main objectives was for Andrew and his classmates to enjoy being together. If they enjoyed it, then it would happen, naturally and more often. Since students use social skills in nearly every aspect of their day, Andrew would have a lot of opportunity to learn. Eventually, Andrew started acquiring these new skills. FRIEND benefitted both Andrew and his classmates. They became more understanding and accepting, and as a result, engaged with him more often. In short, Andrew was now actively integrated with his typical peers.

FRIEND helped Andrew develop social communication and play skills which improved his quality of life and helped him become the quirky, funny employee and community college student he is today.

Friendship builds confidence and provides companionship, emotional support, and opportunities to share interests, hopes, and fears. Parents, teachers, or other school professionals can use FRIEND® for any student in need of social support, regardless of their diagnosis. This manual gets you started and helps you along your way. All pages marked with a ✓ can be downloaded from www.jkp.com/voucher using the code NEYSOJY for your own use.

Sharman Ober-Reynolds, MSN, FNP, CCRP
SARRC Senior Research Coordinator

1

Introduction

All students deserve a positive school experience where they can reach their social and academic potential. However, students with social challenges may struggle daily with confusion in social situations, or experience neglect or bullying by their classmates. For these children, a structured social skills program can create an environment where everyone can do their best. FRIEND® provides opportunities to learn and practice new skills in a structured, supervised, and safe environment. For peers (students without social challenges), FRIEND can teach tolerance, acceptance, and understanding.

Attention deficit, anxiety, and emotional disorders can affect a student's social development. For students with Autism Spectrum Disorder (ASD), social communication impairments are a central component. In all these disorders, students' skills are not on par with those of their classmates in many different areas of functioning, but this is particularly true for social communication. Additionally, students who have very subtle impairments and fall short of meeting full criteria for any of these disorders may still have difficulty making and keeping friends. With the high prevalence of ASD (CDC, 2014), other neurodevelopmental conditions, and subtle impairments affecting social development, teachers will encounter many students who will benefit from a structured social skills program that will improve their chances for reaching full potential. FRIEND provides everything school personnel need to teach and support students with a variety of social challenges in elementary, middle, and high school.

This manual reviews pertinent social skills literature, highlighting the importance of building skills, including play, in a vulnerable student's daily experience. FRIEND describes the characteristics of successful social skill programs and emphasizes how these strategies are incorporated in this manual (Chapter 2). Subsequent chapters outline the steps for successful implementation. First, educators are given tools to recognize and assess a student's social challenges and determine appropriate interventions (Chapter 4). FRIEND® is uniquely designed to support and magnify social skill strategies taught by school professionals throughout the school day and across the school year. FRIEND also educates and motivates peers (Chapter 5) to model, prompt, and provide choice, appropriate praise, and corrective feedback to students with emerging social skills at lunch (Chapter 6) and on the playground (Chapter 7). Since FRIEND is implemented in the natural school setting, as well as at home and in the community, opportunities to learn, practice, and generalize social communication skills are magnified (Chapter 8).

FRIEND®

FRIEND includes three components that can be implemented individually or in any combination as a comprehensive program. This program can complement other social skills curriculum such as video modeling or Social Stories™ but it is not intended to replace an intensive behavioral intervention program for students with ASD. Rather, skills introduced through intervention can be practiced and developed in a supportive, structured environment during non-academic times of the day, like recess and lunch periods. The three components are:

1. Peer Sensitivity Program (PSP)

    i. impacts awareness and understanding of ASD, other disorders, and subtle social challenges

    ii. provides strategies for typical peers and school faculty to support students with social challenges.

2. FRIEND Lunch Program (FLP)

    i. creates a structured Lunch Group that consists of one student with social challenges and same-age, typically developing peers

    ii. provides opportunities for students to develop and practice appropriate social communication skills.

3. FRIEND Playground Program (FPP)

    i.   creates an inclusive environment by facilitating fun, structured activities to the typically unstructured playground

   ii.   provides social coaching and modeling to students with social challenges on the playground, and an opportunity to practice appropriate social communication and play behaviors.

WHO WILL USE THIS MANUAL?

FRIEND® is designed to support any student with social challenges, no matter how subtle. The strategies are implemented by a team of individuals, including educators, therapists, and family members, who are invested in the success of a student with social challenges. For students with a condition that requires an individualized education plan (IEP) such as ASD, FRIEND is best implemented when all members of the IEP team are involved. While some areas of this manual may be clearly directed to specific individuals, it is vital that every team member understands each person's role. Provided below are suggested roles for each possible team member.

Administrator

School administrators set the tone for the social landscape at their schools. Their meaningful leadership can support inclusion for all students with social challenges and provide opportunities for these students to become integral members of the school community. Through FRIEND, a school administrator increases the chance that no student attends school feeling isolated, alone, or without a friend.

Parent

More than anyone, parents want to see their child overcome social challenges. In fact, motivated parents often introduce FRIEND to the school. As a pivotal member of their child's IEP or another support team, parents can be proactive in attending and requesting meetings as necessary. Parents are in the best position to help school employees better understand their child's interests, and how to prepare for success at school.

Parents, and their child with social challenges, may help decide which classmates would be a good fit for FRIEND®. Beyond a child's classroom, parents may know of neighbors, scouts, or children in other classrooms who know and care about their son or daughter. These naturally occurring relationships can help build a successful FRIEND program.

After the team and suitable peers are selected, parents can review and modify FRIEND goals and individualize them according to their child's interests. At the same time, school staff can identify peers' interests so that parents can prime and practice skills at home. For example, if a peer group is interested in a specific television program it would be helpful for the family to watch and chat about the program at home, then the child is better prepared to talk about the show with peers at school. The school will also be collecting and sharing data with parents about their child's progress. This is a time to determine strategies to improve the program, celebrate successes, and acknowledge the hard work of all team members.

School psychologist/counselor

School psychologists and counselors are in an ideal position to implement and support FRIEND. Their training in therapeutic relationship-building techniques and data collection skills are essential to the success of FRIEND. By contacting parents and school personnel to set up a meeting with the IEP/support team (if there is one) a psychologist can get FRIEND started for students on their caseload. The documents in Appendix I can help get the process underway.

Teacher (special or general education)

From the first day of school teachers are observers and soon come to recognize students' strengths and challenges. A teacher's awareness of the dynamic interactions among students is invaluable in determining where social skills may be breaking down. Educators spend the greatest amount of time with students and have the opportunity to ensure that appropriate supports are available across different settings and activities. By ensuring that skill-building opportunities occur throughout the school day, educators can maximize learning and generalization of skills. Teachers are in a pivotal position to model appropriate behavior, prompt, and encourage paraprofessionals and peers to be active members of the FRIEND team.

Therapist (speech language pathologist/ occupational therapist/physical therapist)

Speech and occupational therapists will also have a caseload of students who may benefit from FRIEND®. While anyone who is invested in the student's well-being can start FRIEND, professionals can be instrumental in developing and leading this program. Speech and occupational therapists may be called upon to train school staff and peers to utilize specific strategies when interacting with students who have social challenges (see Appendix V for "Tip Sheets" for peers, facilitators, and teachers). The clinical hours allotted for a given student may be used to oversee FRIEND's implementation or provide direct support to a student as needed (see Chapters 6 and 7).

Paraprofessional

Paraprofessionals are in a position to provide daily support to target students and peers at lunch and on the playground. As guided by the teacher, therapist, or psychologist, paraprofessionals utilize strategies to facilitate communication between students, creating as many opportunities for interaction as possible. With training, a paraprofessional may also be responsible for collecting observational data on target behaviors as determined by the psychologist or therapist. By taking accurate data, the team is able to monitor the progress of the program by analyzing successes and problem solving if necessary (Chapter 4).

CHAPTER SUMMARY

✓ FRIEND can be helpful in every elementary, middle, and high school where students struggle with social challenges. Without interventions, these vulnerable students are often isolated, confused, and ostracized. Through peer sensitivity, education, and support, FRIEND creates an inclusive, safe atmosphere where all students learn strategies for participation and skill-building.

✓ Careful assessment allows FRIEND interventions to be tailored for each student. Ongoing data collection ensures that teaching strategies are appropriate, focused, and updated as needed. Structured implementation of activities at lunch and recess provides multiple and ongoing opportunities for students with social challenges to learn and practice new social communication, and play skills. At the same time, typical peers develop tolerance and leadership.

✓ Parents contribute to FRIEND®'s success by sharing what motivates their child and extending FRIEND interventions at home and in the community, assisting in the generalization of skills. Parents may know of neighbors, friends from scouts, sports, or special interests groups who want to participate in FRIEND.

✓ The information in this manual provides the most comprehensive model for implementing FRIEND. Its appendices provide a wealth of helpful documents to keep the program running smoothly. We realize that just as individuals vary, so do schools, and it may not be possible, or necessary, to implement all strategies identified in this manual. Therefore, FRIEND can be modified to suit the individual and each school environment.

2

The Benefits of FRIEND®s

Three fourth grade students were sitting in a circle on the playground, building a volcano in the sand. They were laughing, joking, and involved in some elaborate pretend play with action figures and the volcano. Charlie, a classmate with ASD, approached the group. Not knowing how to appropriately enter the crowd and game, he stood close by and began kicking the sand around them. When no one from the group took notice of Charlie, he reached down and snatched one of the action figures from a boy's hand. "Hey, go away, you're annoying!" said the boy.

"Yeah, get out of here!" added the girl. Charlie continued to stand above them with the action figure in his hand.

"I SAID, GET OUT OF HERE! You are so annoying!" screamed the boy at Charlie again. The group of kids turned to a playground monitor and all started yelling at once: "Can you make him go away? He is so annoying! Get him away from us!"

At this moment Charlie threw the action figure down in the sand. Before running away from the group Charlie yelled, "I'm not annoying! I'm just lonely!"

FRIENDS FOR LIFE

Charlie's frustration on the playground certainly made him feel badly, but it likely didn't end there. He may have brought those frustrations back to the classroom, which could have interfered with academic activities for him and other classmates. Poor performance in class may have led to increased frustrations and he may have had several behavioral incidents throughout the school day. Charlie's day might have been different if he had had a more positive, supported experience on the playground. Feeling accepted in one area of life can help improve performance in multiple areas.

Imagine that all of the students in a particular school are natural musicians. Each of them improves their natural talent through constant practice. On the playground instead of playing games, they sing or play instruments. There are a small handful of students who are not musical, but they have other interests. The student who plays chess is also tone deaf. While other students practice music, he practices strategic chess moves. When approaching his classmates about chess, they have no interest. When he tries again, with a modest, out-of-tune little song, the other students say he's annoying. After a couple of failed attempts, the chess player doesn't bother to sing at all.

The chess player will only improve his musical skills if he has many opportunities to practice throughout the day, but since the other students find him annoying he actually has fewer opportunities. Because he needs help the school tries to support him, but he only practices once a week for 30 minutes, with an expert musician, in a quiet room away from the harmony of the orchestra. He would likely build his musical skills faster if he was supported while he practiced with the orchestra.

The goal of FRIEND® is to provide integrated interventions in the school setting with the support of typical peers. FRIEND helps close that gap between the limited skills of a student with social challenges and his more experienced classmates. To understand how FRIEND works it's necessary to understand the development of typical social skills.

THE BENEFITS OF EARLY PLAY

Playful behavior emerges in the first few months of life when infants react to caregivers by imitating their sounds and facial expressions (Garvey, 1977). Very young children smile, laugh, and take turns in social games and work hard to keep these interactions going (Lindon, 2001; Ross and Kay, 1980). By six months, babies begin to take notice of other children (Hartup, 1983). By one year, the real excitement for babies is their motivation to go somewhere (Gibson and Pick, 2000).

Toddlers watch and imitate one another, share toys, mimic and respond to one another's emotional cues (Eckerman and Stein, 1982), and begin parallel play. In parallel play children play independently, but with similar play material alongside other children. Later, children establish a common focus in play in which their interactions are loosely organized around shared play activities. This may include socio-dramatic play in which children create imaginative play sequences together.

Even four- and five-year-old children talk about the importance of having friends on the playground (Kernan, 2005). Cooperative play involves complex social organization with shared common goals such as creating an art project, dramatizing an event or playing a formal game (Wolfberg, 2003). By school age, children learn to join other kids in established play. This skill, called peer group entry, enables children to tactfully join other kids in ongoing activities (Dodge *et al.*, 1983). Socially competent kids are considered especially skilled at entering peer groups by hovering on the periphery of the group, imitating and commenting on the activity, and progressively moving closer until they are invited to join (Dodge *et al.*, 1983).

Depending upon the student's current play skills, goals should be selected based on the developmental progression of typical play. Activities selected should be age appropriate. For example, a fifth grade student who is currently engaging in social play may be taught to engage in parallel play activities such as drawing with chalk. The progression of play development is outlined by Pamela Wolfberg in *Peer Play and the Autism Spectrum* (2003). See Table 2.1.

Table 2.1 The progression of play development

Type of play	Example
Social Play	Peek a boo and patty cake
Parallel Play	Digging in the sand next to peers
Early Pretend Play	Playing house with peers
Symbolic-Pretend Play	Making the playground into a jungle with peers
Elaborate Pretend Play	Developing a secret code and playing spies with peers

Adapted from Wolfberg (2003)

During play students learn and practice skills, which lead to gains in cognition, language, literacy, social, emotional, creative, and sensory motor development (Wolfberg, 2003). Table 2.2 illustrates how play contributes to development.

Table 2.2 Play and its relationship to development

Type of play	Skills acquired	Developmental domain
Puzzles, video games, hide and seek, board games, matching games	Knowledge of functional, spatial, causal, categorical relationships; problem solving, mental planning, flexible; and divergent thinking, association, logical memory, and abstract thought	Cognition
Turn-taking games (playground or board games)	Verbal and nonverbal communication, perspective-taking, social awareness; exploration of social roles and issues of intimacy, trust, negotiation, and compromise to form friendship	Social Competence
Play with another person	New vocabulary; forms and functions of language; complex language structures; rules of conversation; metalinguistic awareness (thinking about language)	Language
Reading/writing stories	Interest in stories, knowledge of story structures and story comprehension; narrative competence; understanding of fantasy in books; use of symbols to represent the world	Literacy (Reading and Writing)
Competitive games, team sports	Regulation of affect and emotion; expression of thoughts and feelings; working through emotional conflicts	Emotional Expression
Crafts, imaginative play with figures	Inventiveness, imagination, symbolic representation; enlarged collection of novel ideas and associations	Creative-Artistic Expression
Crafts, tag, catch, riding wheeled toys	Fine- and gross-motor skills; body awareness; sensory regulation	Sensory-Motor

Adapted from Wolfberg (2003)

If a child does not engage in typical play, he or she will have fewer opportunities to develop skills which, like anything that is unpracticed, will inevitably lead to developmental delays.

A core feature of ASD is restricted, repetitive behaviors and interests which can interfere with typical play. Most children with ASD will choose repetitive activities which can limit opportunities for functional or cooperative play. However, when students with ASD are engaged in appropriate interactions and play activities, a decrease in repetitive, stigmatizing behaviors has been reported (Lee, Odom, and Loftin, 2007).

Children with milder social impairments may engage in typical play less often than their peers. Even when given access to space, time, props, and peers, students with social challenges who are not skilled or comfortable in social activities may not be motivated to play or socialize. Consequently, these children are unable to benefit from play or socializing which come naturally to their typically developing peers. Therefore, a comprehensive social skills program should include and support appropriate play for the student with social challenges.

THE BENEFITS OF EARLY SOCIAL NETWORKS

Friendships in childhood lay the groundwork for healthy and satisfying relationships throughout life. True friends bolster feelings of self-worth and provide companionship, emotional support, and opportunities to share interests, hopes, and fears. From our friendships we learn about ourselves and others in the world. Friendships offer opportunities to develop and practice pro-social behaviors such as sharing, caring for one another, cooperation, play skills, empathy, emotional support, and social initiations and responses (Bauminger and Kasari, 2000).

Friendships can help prevent mood disorders by providing a mechanism for emotional monitoring and repair (Hay, Payne, and Chadwick, 2004). Friends can offer guidance on appropriate behavior and help solve problems by providing different perspectives and ideas (Rubin, 2002). Skills that foster friendships and participation in extracurricular activities, such as sociability, punctuality, and conscientiousness, are better predictors of earnings and higher educational achievement than standardized test scores (Lleras, 2008). Finally, the qualities of a good friend are also the qualities of a good employee as well as a lifetime partner (Attwood, 2007).

If a student does not have the skills, or opportunity, to even start a conversation it is difficult to develop a real friendship. The lack of friendships in childhood often leads to depression, anxiety, decreased independent living, and decreased employment (Strain, 1991; Strain and Schwartz, 2001; Wing, 1981). Contrary to the belief that individuals with an ASD prefer to be alone, many indicate they want friends but lack the skills to relate to their peers (Attwood, 2007). As social skills become more complex with age, deficits tend to increase over time likely because of limited opportunities to practice skills (Howlin, Mawhood, and Rutter, 2000). Even with opportunities to practice social skills, an inclusive setting without structure is inadequate for students with significant social delays. Adolescents with ASD attending typical classrooms experience more loneliness, poorer friendship quality, and more isolation than their peers (Locke *et al.*, 2010).

Without the implementation of a comprehensive social skills program, students with social challenges such as ASD are vulnerable and often neglected and rejected by their classmates. According to parent report, most children with ASD are also targets for peer victimization (Little, 2002). Bullying was the most frequent form of victimization, which included emotional and physical bullying, but peer shunning was another common theme. Many students were not invited to birthday parties, ate alone at lunch, and were picked last for teams (Shtayermman, 2007).

STUDENTS WITH SOCIAL CHALLENGES

It is easy to identify a student who has social challenges when they are isolated from their peers on the playground, in the lunchroom, or in the classroom. It is more difficult to identify a student with social differences who is engaging with peers, but in a limited or inappropriate manner. For example, a student with social challenges playing hopscotch with a peer begins to turn the game into a chasing game. The typical peer indicates through verbal and nonverbal communication that they are not interested. The student with social challenges continues with the chase game and the peer walks away. If this interaction is observed from a distance, it may appear like two students playing. However, watching the interaction closely, it is obvious that one student is unable to read social cues and maintain the interaction.

Students with social challenges have difficulty communicating with others, processing and integrating information from the environment, establishing and sustaining social relationships with others, and generalizing skills in new environments. Specific social skill deficits may include difficulty initiating interactions, maintaining reciprocity, sharing enjoyment, taking another person's perspective, and inferring the interests of others. Even students without a diagnosable condition can have social challenges and require support.

SOCIAL PRAGMATICS

Observation of the student with social challenges will provide an opportunity to better understand how they use language in social settings. Traditionally, speech and language pathologists focused on the content and form of language, assuming that when a student has these skills they would use them intuitively. However, individuals with social deficits may be unable to effectively communicate in social settings in spite of having adequate or even advanced language skills (Winner, 2006). Even individuals without ASD have varying levels of expertise when it comes to social pragmatics. Some students seem to be natural communicators, able to easily organize their thoughts and feelings into language others can understand. For a variety of reasons, others struggle.

There are many reasons students with social/communication disorders (SCD) have difficulty chatting with their peers:

- They may not pay attention when one of their classmates is talking because of their classmate's distracting gestures, or other things going on in the classroom or playground.

- If a peer is speaking quickly, using unfamiliar words, talking about something disinteresting or unfamiliar to the student with an SCD, they will likely tune out of the conversation.

- Figurative language may be lost on students with SCD, who tend to use words in a very concrete manner.

- Students with SCD may have only a partial understanding of their peers' point of view. This may limit their ability to respond in a meaningful way.

- Challenges with auditory processing can result in students being overwhelmed with what their peers are saying.

- Even if students with social communication challenges want to respond, they may have trouble articulating their intent because of limited vocabulary or disordered sentence structure.

- Some students with social challenges may be very used to one-turn conversations and not even recognize that a second response is expected. (Vicker, 2009)

Students with social challenges struggle for a variety of reasons. However, no matter what the reason, without intervention social challenges negatively impact a student's quality of life and may eventually lead to long-term mental health consequences and decreased opportunities in adulthood. Recognizing a student's isolated or inappropriate behavior is the first step. In future chapters FRIEND® provides tools educators can use to determine the reasons for a particular student's struggles and focused strategies to teach, practice, and support emerging play, social, and communication skills.

CHAPTER SUMMARY

✓ Play supports the development of the following skills: cognition, social competence, language, literacy, emotional expression, creative-artistic expression, and sensory-motor.

✓ Even when given access to space, time, props, and peers, students with social challenges who are not skilled or comfortable in social activities may not be motivated to play or socialize. FRIEND teaches play skills and increases the motivation, opportunity, and support these students need to be successful.

✓ Friendships offer opportunities to practice and develop skills such as sharing, cooperation, empathy, and emotional support, which make a good employee and lifetime partner.

✓ Lack of friendships in childhood often leads to depression, anxiety, and decreased employment and opportunities to live independently.

✓ The first step in FRIEND is for educators to recognize that a particular student is struggling socially. Future chapters will provide educators with assessment tools and focused strategies for intervention.

3

Intervention Strategies

Dominic hated going to school in the morning. His mother complained that he would put up such a fight when it was time to get ready to leave that he was often late. Dominic's paraprofessional reported that he never greeted her in the morning or played with peers on the playground. After FRIEND® was included in Dominic's IEP she encouraged him to play with typical peers during recess. Within a few weeks of starting the program, he began seeking her out in the morning to say "hi" and ask her what games he and his friends would play on the playground that day. Dominic's mother also reported that he was excited to go to school in the morning. Recess was a small part of Dominic's school day, but when he started to play with peers his whole outlook was changed.

KEEP IT SIMPLE

FRIEND's goals are to teach and support students with social challenges while they learn, practice, and improve their social communication and play skills. Of course, one of the most important goals of FRIEND is to improve the quality of life of these students as well.

The type, quality, and amount of social skill programming are critical factors in producing meaningful change. Peer-mediated programs improved reciprocal interactions with peers (Goldstein, Schneider, and Thiemann, 2007; Kohler *et al.*, 2007; McGee *et al.*, 1992; Owen-DeSchryver *et al.*, 2008), increased interactions during play (Nelson *et al.*, 2007), and increased social initiations and turn taking during recess (Harper, Symon, and Frea, 2008). While these studies demonstrated promising results, other research on social skill programming demonstrated less significant results for students. In a meta-analysis of social skills research Bellini *et al.* (2007) found that the following strategies (Gresham, Sugai, and Horner, 2001) lead to the best outcomes:

- Provide frequent opportunities to teach and reinforce social skills throughout the school day rather than limit them to isolated therapy sessions.

- Provide interventions that can be reasonably implemented in multiple naturalistic settings.

- Match the intervention strategy with the type of skill deficit (see Chapter 4).

- Ensure implementation fidelity because a poorly implemented program will decrease its effectiveness.

- Ensure social validity of the program. Teachers, parents, and peers need to believe in the social objectives of the program. That is, when the student's IEP team believes that the intervention makes sense, they will more likely implement the program as intended.

There are a variety of interventions designed to teach social skills; a review of the literature indicates which strategies are most effective (see below). FRIEND® applies elements from each strategy as shown in Table 3.1.

Table 3.1 FRIEND®'s application of evidence-based practice

Evidence-based practice	FRIEND program
1. Naturalistic environment	Designed to take place at lunch, at recess, before/after school, in the community
2. Naturalistic procedures	Uses natural reinforcers and student choices, and incorporates student interests in the natural environment
3. Peer mediated	Peers are vital to the program, by teaching, modeling, reinforcing, and supporting the student with ASD, or other social challenges
4. Frequency of implementation	Intervention provided daily
5. Student directed	Activities and games the FRIEND group participates in should utilize the interests of the student with ASD, or other social challenges

6. Cooperative arrangements	Activities and games during intervention can be designed and structured into cooperative arrangements
7. Mutually reinforcing	Students who have common interests with the student with social challenges may be encouraged to participate in the FRIEND® program. Games and activities selected for intervention should include the interests of all FRIEND group members
8. Match intervention to deficit	Following a thorough assessment of the student with social challenges, strategies to teach desired skills should match the type of deficit determined
9.Generalization/ maintenance	Intervention provided in the natural environment increases maintenance and generalization of skills

1. NATURALISTIC ENVIRONMENT

The Education for All Handicapped Children Act (1975) mandated that public schools must educate students with special needs in the least restrictive environment. That is, special needs students needed to be included in classrooms with typically developing peers. As a result, the inclusion of students with academic and social challenges in general education classrooms became more common. The reauthorization of the Individuals with Disabilities Education Act (IDEA) in 1997, and again in 2004, placed an emphasis on access to the general curriculum for all students. Inclusion is associated with improved social behavior (Strain, Odom, and McConnell, 1984), maintenance and generalization effects (Bellini *et al.*, 2007), and emotional, cognitive, and speech development (Hume, Bellini, and Pratt, 2005).

Inclusion provided the framework for progressive treatment of students with various challenges, including ASD. Children with developmental delays needed more exposure, not less, to typically developing children to foster their own development. However, exposure is often not enough without additional support, which is why special needs children often are provided with an aide who helps them in the classroom. Without proper support, physically integrating students may not produce the desired outcomes, such as increased social skills or academics (Gresham, 1984; Kamps *et al.*, 1998). While aides can adapt the curriculum to help the child be successful in the classroom, there are no federal mandates to require support on the playground. These students had no support to overcome social impairments which can limit their functioning as much as academic difficulties.

Through inclusion, students with social challenges participate with peers in their naturalistic or typical environment. However, some naturalistic environments are more therapeutic than others. The best environment (typical classroom, playground, or lunchroom) includes staff members trained in various supportive strategies.

School-based social skills programs that involved pull-out settings (i.e. resource room or therapy room) led to poor generalization and maintenance of skills (Bellini et al., 2007). However, programs implemented in the typical classroom were more effective and led to better generalization and maintenance of skills. Other studies also demonstrate the benefits of teaching social skills in a typical naturalistic setting, such as on the playground or lunchroom (Baker, Koegel, and Koegel, 1998; Harper et al., 2008; Owen-DeSchryver et al., 2008). Thus, the use of typical naturalistic settings when implementing social skills interventions is recommended. FRIEND® is implemented within the context of a student's natural environment at lunch or recess.

2. NATURALISTIC PROCEDURES

Beyond typical naturalistic settings, it is also important to incorporate elements in the setting that are motivating to the student. Loosely structured programs that are influenced by the students' interests are generally more effective than adult-directed, rigid settings. Ingersoll and Schreibman (2006) used naturalistic procedures to teach reciprocal imitation skills to students with ASD, which were successfully generalized to novel environments. The students also demonstrated increased social behaviors, such as language, pretend play, and joint attention.

A body of research indicates the positive effects of having children choose what motivates them in a naturalistic environment. Pivotal response teaching (PRT) is an intervention designed to focus on specific "pivotal behaviors" that can impact global functioning (Koegel, Carter, and Koegel, 2003). A critical element of PRT is allowing students to make a choice among elements of a task (how to approach, where to complete it, who to talk to, which toy to play with) whenever possible to help maintain their motivation on a given task. The choices made by the student, or natural reinforcers, can be paired with social responses like praise, or high-fives, to increase the child's motivation from social interaction.

When students' focused interests were incorporated into social games on the playground, social interaction, joint attention, and generalization of skills improved (Baker *et al.*, 1998; Baker, 2000). These pivotal studies used the interests of students with autism to create socially appropriate games. For example, one student was interested in animated characters so they created a game that involved elements related to these characters. They also created movie- and geography-themed tag games using the interests of other students with social challenges. These studies demonstrated the development of appropriate social skills as a result of student choice.

Student choice can also help reduce inappropriate social behaviors such as looking away, closing eyes, or moving away (Koegel, Dyer, and Bell, 1987). Researchers found that children could initiate preferred activities with little prompting (e.g. find somebody to play with). They followed up by using the same procedures to teach children to initiate student-preferred activities in the community, and successfully removed all prompts while the children maintained the skill.

Interventions that include student choice may be effective in part because individuals with learning or social challenges are often not given opportunities to express preferences. Some negative results of not offering choices may include learned helplessness. The opportunity to express preferences and make choices may lead to improved quality of life (Kern *et al.*, 1998).

Peers invited to join a FRIEND® group might include students who have similar interests as the student with social challenges. Also, activities offered on the playground or during FRIEND group meetings may be designed around the interest of the student with ASD, as Baker *et al.* (1998) demonstrated. Peers who participate in FRIEND can be encouraged to offer choices to their classmates as an intervention to increase positive social behaviors.

3. PEER MEDIATED

Students with social challenges do not learn social skills from interactions as well as their typical peers. Since learning does not occur naturally (or at the same rate) it *needs* to be explicitly taught (Harper *et al.*, 2008). Therefore, it is imperative that social skills be strategically individualized with a structured and supportive program like FRIEND. Peer-mediated instruction is considered to be an emerging and effective strategy to teach play to children with ASD (Odom *et al.*, 2003).

FRIEND® strategies also benefit typical peers by teaching valuable social skills and encouraging them to expand their own social networks. Peer-mediated social support interventions provide peers with opportunities for personal growth, greater understanding of self, greater appreciation of diversity, advocacy skills, and lasting friendships (e.g. Carter *et al.*, 2001; Copeland *et al.*, 2004; Hughes *et al.*, 2001; Kamps *et al.*, 1998; Kishi and Meyer, 1994). However, typical peers require guidance to develop friendships involving students with social challenges. The following strategies can enrich the environment for teaching friendship at school (Powers and Powers, 2000):

- It's best to acknowledge shortcomings and recognize strengths.

- Students readily notice strengths and shortcomings among each other, with themselves, and with their classmates with special needs. When students can identify a special ability or interest in a child with ASD, or other social differences, that child has power.

- FRIEND will encourage peers to recognize the shortcomings of a student with social challenges and help them to adapt, as well as appreciate their strengths.

- Peers need an invitation to be a friend.

- Most typical peers are willing and excited about helping another student, but often do not know how to begin. Given appropriate strategies, typical peers are empowered to support a student with social challenges. These skills are the foundation for lasting friendships.

- We learn best by example.

- FRIEND encourages a culture of understanding, compassion, humor, and creative problem solving that involves parents, staff, and students. The commitment of parents and staff provides an example to the typical peers who in turn provide an example to the rest of the class to support the student with social challenges. As a result, a rich learning environment is created.

Developing a sense of competence in typical peers is critical to the success of an inclusive social skill program. Typical peers need strategies to be helpful and engage a student with social challenges. They also need to know how to respond to the student's attempt at socialization. FRIEND teaches these valuable skills.

While FRIEND® is primarily implemented during recess and lunch, its principles can have an effect on the rest of the school day as well. Students with social challenges develop better skills and their typical peers learn to respond more positively, leading to greater self-respect and self-determination throughout the school day. As typical peers are proactive and supportive to the student with challenges, dependence on aid support decreases and the student is less stigmatized. All students experience a greater sense of class membership and belonging.

FRIEND is most effective when goals address both the quantity and quality of all students' interactions. It's helpful to measure the change in behavior of the student with social differences, as well as changes in peers' behavior. Table 3.2 describes skills that can be targeted as part of FRIEND implementation.

The Observation Recording Form, a tool used to measure the qualities of student interaction, is included in Appendix IV.

Table 3.2 Goals in social skills programming

Initiations from student
One critical social skill is the ability to initiate social interactions with typical classmates (Kalyva and Avramidis, 2005; McGee et al., 1992; Owen-Desschryver et al., 2008). Such initiations may include asking a peer a question, commenting on a task completed together, or any other vocal or motor behavior specifically directed toward another student, with the expectation of a response.
Initiations, whether verbal or nonverbal, are a stepping stone toward future social success. Imagine a student without the ability to request a desired item or ask to join in with a group of kids. Without this skill, school can be very lonely and isolating. The lack of this skill may also lead to undesirable behaviors in an effort to communicate a desire or need. For example, a student who is unable to initiate appropriately with a peer who has a desired toy or item, may just reach and grab for the toy. Thus, an undesirable interaction may escalate, leaving the student with ASD or another social challenge facing a possible meltdown, timeout, or other consequences. This interaction might prevent the peer from wanting to interact with the student with social challenges.
Responses of peers
While a student may initiate appropriately with peers, he or she will not continue to initiate in the future if peers do not respond positively to these initiations. It is important to be aware not only of students' initiations but also the responses that follow.
Students with social challenges who begin to learn and understand the importance of effective social interaction skills can be devastated when they try out their new skills in environments that are insensitive and unsupportive. Their sense of excitement deflates the moment their social overtures are unwittingly rejected by their peers.

cont.

Engagement with peers

In addition to appropriate initiations, another skill is the ability to maintain a reciprocal interaction (Harper *et al.*, 2008; Kalyva and Avramidis, 2005; Kamps *et al.*, 2002; Kohler *et al.*, 1997; Kohler *et al.*, 2007; McGee *et al.*, 1992). This includes responding appropriately to the approaches of another student by answering a question, providing a requested item, or engaging in another appropriate behavior in response to an initiation from another student.

Engagement refers to the length of time an interaction with another student lasts, which includes both initiations and responses. Engagement has been reported to increase after participation in inclusive social skill interventions (Kamps *et al.*, 2002).

Initiations from peers

It is also important to observe and measure the frequency of initiations that peers make to the student with social differences. As the student begins to interact more appropriately with peers, the number of peers initiating should increase. This is an appropriate measure of how well peers are accepting that individual into their peer groups.

Peers, who may have initiated with this student in the past, may have not received an appropriate response and therefore stopped initiating with that student. Peers should be encouraged to initiate with that student in the future so that an appropriate response can be given and initiations will continue in the future.

Responses from student

Often, a student with social differences will either not respond, or respond inappropriately, to their classmates, thus decreasing these initiations in the future. These students need practice and support on how to give appropriate responses.

Imagine that you are waiting in a crowd for an event and you decide to make a nice comment or gesture toward another person nearby about the event. What do you think if that person looks at you oddly, walks away, or completely ignores you? Most likely, if you see this person again, you won't bother approaching him or her, given that your past experience was unsuccessful.

Typically developing children are constantly making initiations to each other, whether it is to ask for something, talking about their day, or inviting someone to play. If they approach a student with social challenges but receive an inappropriate response, such as an odd statement (maybe a scripted phrase from a favorite movie), or the student walks away or ignores the approach, the typical child may begin to lose interest. It is possible that the student with social challenges is interested in the interaction, but does not know how to respond appropriately. As the child with social challenges develops his or her ability to respond appropriately to his or her peers, opportunities for interactions may naturally increase, which can lead to friendships.

While all friendships have their value, the skills that each student brings to the friendship can make interactions more rewarding. Consider three kinds of friendships: typical, mixed, and non-mixed. Typical friendships include two typically developing peers; mixed friendships include a student with ASD and a typical peer; and non-mixed include two students with ASD. Investigating the dynamics of each friendship revealed that typical friends influence the quality of the interaction. In mixed friendships students with ASD exhibited better receptive language, complex coordinated play, responsiveness, and higher levels of positive social orientation than students with ASD in non-mixed friendships (Bauminger *et al.*, 2008).

4. FREQUENCY OF IMPLEMENTATION

While it makes sense that a more effective program is implemented more frequently than one that only involves an hour a week, many studies did not provide adequate information regarding the length and duration of the interventions (Bellini *et al.*, 2007). Frequent opportunities to teach and reinforce social skills are recommended (Gresham *et al.*, 2001). Rather than schedule allotted time for social skills training, it is recommended that parents, teachers, paraprofessionals, and therapists look for opportunities to teach and reinforce appropriate social skills throughout the natural course of the day.

5. STUDENT DIRECTED

Choices improve motivation and decrease problem behaviors in children with ASD (Koegel and LaZebnik, 2004). An overarching theme of FRIEND® is the importance of identifying and embedding students' interests in programming and interventions. On the playground students choose activities and who they will play with. Students are involved in identifying who they will eat lunch with, and to some degree, shared conversational topics in the FLP.

At home, parents learn to integrate learning opportunities in ongoing, motivating play, personal chores, or self-help activities. While a socially challenged student will not have the option of remaining isolated at school or home, they will be able to make many and ongoing choices about how, where, and with whom they interact. Providing choices offers students with social challenges dignity and independence. Choices can also distract students from their perseverations and limiting anxiety.

6. COOPERATIVE ARRANGEMENTS

In cooperative play, each student has a say in the activity, and everyone is having fun. Researchers have found that cooperative play arrangements can be helpful in increasing the frequency of interactions among individuals with and without disabilities (Hyten and Burns, 1986; Kennedy and Itkonen, 1996). The participants learn to complete a project together while supporting each other with encouragement and praise, as well as ensuring that each member of the group contributes to the project as a whole. Often, the group receives a group reward, or reinforcement, upon completion of the common goal.

Koegel *et al.* (2005) used cooperative arrangements as part of supported play dates to promote reciprocal interactions and improve affect. Overall, it was necessary for each student to participate and work together to create a positive and rewarding outcome. For younger children an adult can serve as a facilitator to promote interactions and ensure cooperation from everyone involved.

In our example at the beginning of this chapter, Charlie could benefit from FRIEND®. Once in the program, his group could set up several cooperative arrangements for him in the classroom, on the playground and even at home. Table 3.3 shows what these arrangements might look like.

Table 3.3 An example of cooperative arrangements

What to do	School art class	Playground	Play date
Preparation	Decide on a project everyone likes Briefly train typical peers to: model, prompt, and provide choice, appropriate praise, and corrective feedback to student with social challenges (SC)	Observe favorite playground activities: building volcanoes in sandbox Provide typical peers with strategies to: model, prompt, and provide choice, appropriate praise, and corrective feedback to student with SC	Invite a child for a play date with a shared interest in cooking Encourage typical peer to: model, prompt, and provide choice, appropriate praise, and corrective feedback to student with SC

Set the stage	Encourage students to describe common goal: prehistoric collage Give each child different materials (paper, glue, crayons, glitter) so they interact to complete the art project	Encourage students to describe their activities: volcanoes and general mayhem with action figures Give each child a different action figure and tools to dig in the sand so they interact in the sandbox	Have students decide on goal: dinosaur cookies Give one child the measuring cup and another the sugar. One child can crack the eggs while the other stirs the cookie dough
Supervision	Leaders provide relevant instruction, and encourage interaction and cooperation	Aide encourages interaction and cooperation	Parent encourages interaction and cooperation

7. MUTUALLY REINFORCING

Koegel *et al.* (2005) investigated the effects of supported play dates (versus play dates without supports) to promote reciprocal interactions and improve affect. During the play dates without supports, the children were responsible for choosing their own activity (both indoor and outdoor were available) and engaging without instruction. There were two components of supports: 1) selected activities chosen to cater to the shared interests of both children; and 2) cooperative arrangements set up by an adult within each activity. Results of the supported play dates were increased reciprocal interactions and positive affect for both the peer and student with autism, and increased invitations from the peer to come over and play, as reported by the parents.

In order to select the appropriate peer and activity for such play dates, the researchers spent time informally observing the student with ASD in natural settings, in addition to consultation with the teacher and parents to determine possible playmates. Specifically, playmates with positive social behaviors and similar interests were asked to participate in the play dates. The same process was utilized to determine activities that would be of interest to both children during the play date.

Selecting activities that will be motivating and of interest to all children involved may help increase joint participation and social conversation.

Most importantly, this may ensure that all of the children involved have fun during the activity, therefore increasing momentum to interact together and participate in other activities in the future (Werner *et al.*, 2006).

8. MATCH INTERVENTION TO DEFICIT

It is important to individualize an intervention to target a specific skill deficit. For example, there are acquisition deficits and performance deficits and each can impair a student's social functioning. An acquisition deficit refers to the absence of a particular skill or behavior. If a student has never, under any circumstances, initiated a conversation, then it's likely that the student does not have that skill. Performance deficits refer to a skill or behavior that is present, but not used appropriately. A student with social challenges may know how to start a conversation with another student but doesn't because of anxiety, lack of motivation, or sensory challenges.

Gresham *et al.* (2001) reviewed several studies of social skills training, which yielded results ranging from ineffective to highly effective. Based on the review, they determined that the ineffectiveness of many interventions may have been due to a failure to match the intervention to the skill deficit. A meta-analysis of school-based social skills interventions (Bellini *et al.*, 2007) revealed only one study which described the type of skill deficit the participant demonstrated.

In another review of several social skill treatments Matson, Matson, and Rivet (2007) noted that in all of the studies reviewed, no justification for the selection of target behaviors was addressed. Given that children with social challenges may exhibit a complex variety of skill deficits, it would be inappropriate to assume all children require the same intervention for the same set of target skills. It is also possible that some skills may need to be learned prior to learning another skill in order to maximize a student's effective functioning and social behavior. The authors argue for "more systematic methods of identifying [social skill] behaviors to ensure that the skill most likely to benefit the individual is targeted for intervention first" (p.695). Before determining the intervention to put into place, it is clear that the appropriate target behavior should be determined based on a full assessment.

9. GENERALIZATION/MAINTENANCE

Generalization of skills is an integral component of social skills interventions and programming. Additionally, the success of any social skills curriculum or intervention should be based on the student's ability to maintain and generalize a learned skill or behavior. Generalization is the ability of a student to perform a learned skill or behavior in different settings with many different people.

If a student has learned to initiate a greeting, but can only greet a parent when at home, the skill is not truly mastered. Generalization has occurred when that student can successfully greet a variety of people through his or her day, such as peers and teachers at school, the bus driver on the school bus, neighbors, and family members. When determining which intervention to use when designing a specific social skills curriculum, it is very important to incorporate generalization and maintenance of learned skills into the planning. FRIEND® strategies will help in such a plan. For instance, providing intervention in natural settings will allow the student to learn to perform skills in his or her desired environments many times each day.

Peer-mediated interventions may also increase generalization effects as the student learns to perform skills among multiple peers. Hall and Smith (1996) investigated the use of preferred peers during intervention. The study demonstrates that when children with ASD indicated a preference for peers, their performance during interventions may be increased.

INCORPORATING OTHER SOCIAL SKILLS INTERVENTIONS

FRIEND can be used in conjunction with other social skills interventions including: video modeling (a form of observational learning in which desired behaviors are learned by watching a video and then imitated), Social Thinking (Winner, 2000), speech interventions, Super Skills (Coucouvanis, 2005) and Hidden Curriculum (Myles, Trautman, and Schelvan, 2004). These interventions often target social skills in a more structured setting and then generalize to the natural environment. These types of interventions can be great for teaching and practicing appropriate social skills, which can be generalized on the playground or in the lunchroom as part of FRIEND.

POSITIVE BEHAVIOR SUPPORT

FRIEND® strategies may also improve the culture at a school by encouraging positive behavior support (PBS). While PBS was initially designed to decrease challenging behavior and increase socially appropriate behavior, it is now applied to all students throughout the school day Colvin *et al.*, 1997).

School-wide PBS utilizes three levels of intervention to effectively change the behavior of all students within the school setting. The primary prevention is a universal intervention system used to improve behavior of all students. The secondary prevention is an intervention designed to target students at risk for problem behavior. The tertiary prevention is an individualized intervention designed for one individual student with intense problematic behaviors (Sugai, Horner, and Sprague, 1999).

FRIEND follows a PBS model by increasing social skills of individuals, fostering the development of relationships, and preventing problematic behaviors. The peer sensitivity component of the FRIEND program is a primary prevention because it is a school-wide curriculum. The playground component is designed to be available to all students on the playground, with a specific emphasis on students with social challenges, making this a secondary prevention. The lunch program is a tertiary prevention, designed to be an individualized social skills intervention to assist students who need a significant amount of support to improve their social skills and build meaningful friendships.

Social skill development begins with early play and continues throughout childhood, elementary school years, adolescence, and even adulthood. Each stage of development presents new social challenges and requires new opportunities to learn and practice developing skills. FRIEND helps educators recognize the needs of students with social challenges and provides effective strategies to teach social communication, and play skills throughout a student's day and across the school year.

CHAPTER SUMMARY

✓ Over the past few decades, the inclusion of students with autism in general education classrooms has become a growing and positive trend among public schools.

✓ Benefits of inclusion in general classrooms include learning appropriate social behavior and higher maintenance and generalization of skills. However, integrating students without adequate support may not produce the desired outcomes.

✓ Supported peer-mediated interventions are an effective strategy to improve social communication and play skills for individuals with social challenges.

✓ An effective FRIEND® program will be implemented in the natural environment, rely on natural motivators, be peer mediated, be implemented at lunch and on the playground so students with social challenges have many opportunities to learn and practice skills, and ensure games and activities are fun and motivating for all students.

✓ FRIEND follows a PBS model by increasing social skills of individuals, fostering the development of relationships, and preventing problematic behaviors.

4

Data Drives FRIEND®

I have worked with many schools that had students in need of a social support program but didn't know where to begin. The individual student is usually the place to start. FRIEND® works best when tailored to the individual.

Standardized questionnaires may help to measure a student's social challenges and identify the need for support but lend little information as to the cause of the challenges. To really identify challenges and strengths I encourage the staff to observe the student's interactions closely. Some students may be around peers, but not interacting. Other students may be engaged with peers, but the interactions may not be appropriate or sustained. Direct observation with a careful, knowledgeable eye is best.

GETTING STARTED

Data driven decisions are essential to FRIEND. Data collection can determine differences in a student's social functioning when compared with peers or normative samples and can justify the need for FRIEND. Then, once the program begins, qualitative data can help identify the root of the problem and specific skills that need to be developed. Baseline data on target skills should be collected so that progress can be documented. Follow-up data on those same skills will inform the FRIEND team that the program is working, or needs adjustment. From start to finish, FRIEND is heavily dependent on data collection. This chapter provides information on assessments that can guide the way for any school that is interested in incorporating FRIEND.

As FRIEND® relies on both quantitative and qualitative data, it is an ideal program for students that have an IEP indicating a need for social supports. A good IEP should also rely on data. FRIEND encourages staff and parents to work together to decide on an appropriate plan to teach relevant skills and support the student. The right assessments can help inform this process. Through assessments, strengths can be an asset in the planning of FRIEND, challenges can be measured, interventions implemented, and improvement documented. Suggestions for conducting initial assessments, goal development, and planning are outlined in this chapter.

SCHOOL GUIDELINES

School districts may have guidelines regarding which assessments are approved for use and who is qualified to administer the assessments. Another consideration is where data will be securely stored. For example, will assessment data be part of an IEP, 504 (a plan to ensure appropriate accommodations for students with disabilities), or Functional Behavioral Assessment? If the student has milder social impairments, and not a formal diagnosis, where will records be maintained? Each school will have its own policies for securing parental permission, data collection, and storage. The FRIEND team will want to ensure that school policies are understood and followed.

WHO SHOULD COLLECT DATA?

A careful assessment can help the team determine what, where, when, and how the student will be taught social skills. Early in the process (or at an IEP meeting), the FRIEND team should identify the following:

- appropriate quantitative scales to measure differences from peers
- appropriate qualitative questionnaires to best reflect challenges
- appropriate structured interviews with parents, if necessary
- raters to collect observational data for baseline and progress
- a coordinator to guide the whole process.

This collaborative process also creates the expectation and opportunity for all members of the team to work together. Observational data will also provide information about the student's environment, specifically how peers respond to the student. Working together and communicating results from assessments will provide the most comprehensive picture of the student.

STANDARDIZED ASSESSMENT OF GENERAL SOCIAL SKILLS

Standardized rating scales can be helpful when confirming that a student's social functioning is significantly different from that of his or her peers. Scales can measure global functioning, such as socialization, and even more focused components such as: cooperation, assertion, responsibility, empathy, self-control, behavioral challenges, self-esteem, adaptive skills, academic achievement, and anxiety. These measures compare the student's skills with the general population of peers and are good ways to identify students who need support and justify the application of FRIEND®, but due to their global approach to skills their application to planning a program is limited, as shown in Table 4.1.

Table 4.1 Advantages and disadvantages of standardized rating scales

Description of Scale	Advantages	Disadvantages
Applicability	Can identify global measures of: • social functioning • anxiety • self-esteem • behavioral functioning	Not all rating scales are standardized for individuals with specific disorders or social challenges
Psychometric	Rating scales are well-standardized, reliable, and valid	Lack of sensitivity: the incremental gains often seen in students may not be measurable on standardized scales
Meaningful	Rating scales establish a "score" which can be meaningful to clinicians and researchers who know the tool	Individuals can score within normal limits, but it does not mean that skills are used appropriately
Effect of scoring	Rating scales can help establish baseline data for a typical skill	Parents and educators may focus on the significant social challenges identified by a particular tool instead of possible areas to intervene

In fact, if the student has an obvious impairment or a diagnosis (ASD) it may not be necessary to conduct any of these assessments. The scales shown in Table 4.2 were developed to measure social functioning of the general population. This table can help the educator decide which scale is most appropriate to an individual student.

Table 4.2 Scales to measure social functioning of the general population

Name	Author	Age	Time	Description of tool
Social Responsiveness Scale (SRS)	Constantino and Gruber 2005	4–18	15–20 minutes	This 65-item rating scale measures the severity of autism spectrum symptoms as they occur in natural social settings Completed by a parent or teacher, the SRS provides a clear picture of a child's social impairments, assessing social awareness, social information processing, capacity for reciprocal social communication, social anxiety/avoidance, and autistic preoccupations and traits
Social Skills Improvement System (SSIS)	Gresham and Elliot, 2008	3–18	10–20 minutes	The SSIS rating scale enables targeted assessment of individuals to evaluate social skills, problem behaviors, and academic competence Teacher, parent, and student forms help provide a comprehensive picture across school, home, and community settings
Multidimensional Anxiety Scale for Children (MASC)	March et al., 1999	8–19	5–10 minutes	This 45-item instrument provides an assessment of anxiety symptoms across multiple dimensions, such as Physical Symptoms, Social Anxiety, Harm Avoidance, and Separation/Panic

Social Anxiety Scale for Children (SAS-C) and Adolescents (SAS-A)	La Greca, 1999	6–19	5–10 minutes	The SAS is a self-report measure of social anxiety consisting of three factors: Fear of Negative Evaluation, Social Avoidance and Distress in New Situations, and Social Avoidance and Distress-General
Behavioral Assessments Scale for Children (BASC)	Reynolds and Kamphaus, 1992	2–21	10–20 minutes	This is a multidimensional measure using teacher, parent, and self-report to assess anxiety, social skill problems, and other behaviors There is also a 20-minute interview for children ages 6–7
Adaptive Behavior Assessment System – Second Edition (ABAS-II)	Harrison and Oakland, 2003	Birth to 89	15–20 minutes	This scale can be completed by parents, family members, or teachers and assesses adaptive behavior, or what people actually do without the assistance of others
Multidimensional Self-Concept Scale (MSCS)	Bracken, 1992	9–19	20 minutes	The MSCS assesses global self-concept and six self-concept domains that are important in the social-emotional adjustment of youth and adolescents The six domains assessed by the MSCS include: Social, Competence, Affect, Academic, Family, and Physical Each of these primary domains can be assessed independently by administering any of the six 25-item scales, or when administered in combination the six scales comprise a 150-item assessment of the child's global self-concept

cont.

Name	Author	Age	Time	Description of tool
The Autism Social Skills Profile (ASSP)	Bellini, 2006a	6–17	10–20 minutes	The items on the ASSP collect data from a child's parents, or other family members, on a broad range of social challenges typically seen in children with ASD including initiation skills, reciprocity, perspective taking, and nonverbal communication

LANGUAGE-BASED ASSESSMENTS

Language is an important element of social functioning and impairments may result in diminished opportunities to learn and practice social skills. Treating specific language impairments, however, will not replace the missed social learning opportunities. FRIEND® will provide the opportunity to practice and develop social skills with greater frequency than would occur during the typical school day. The scales in Table 4.3 can help determine impairments related to language and, unlike many standardized assessments that measure global constructs, some of these scales can be used to measure progress of a specific student. These scales are best administered and interpreted by a speech and language pathologist.

Table 4.3 Language assessment scales

Name	Publisher	Age	Time	Description
The Test of Pragmatic Language-2 (TOPL-2)	Phelps-Terasaki and Phelps-Gunn, 2007	6–18	45–60 minutes	This assessment provides an in-depth and comprehensive analysis of social communication in context. Its four principal uses include: identifying individuals with pragmatic language deficits, determining individual strengths and weaknesses, documenting an individual's progress, and researching pragmatic language skills

Test of Problem Solving Adolescent (TOPS-A)	Bowers, Huisingh, and LoGiudice, 2007	12–17	35–40 minutes	The TOPS-A is an open-ended test for adolescents, who are asked to critically analyze a written passage, much of which is socially oriented
				The assessment encourages students to recognize the gestalt summary of the scenario, interpret the meaning, and then give their own responses to specific questions
				Even if students with ASD score within normal limits, the test often reveals unconventional answers
Test of Problem Solving-Elementary, Revised (TOPS-E, Revised)	Zachman, *et al.*, 1994	6–12	35 minutes	In this open-ended test the information is presented through pictures that portray the scenarios
				The student looks at the pictures and then answers questions about the content
				This format may be easier for students with ASD to complete
Comprehensive Assessment of Spoken Language (CASL)	Carrow-Woolfolk, 1999	3–22	30–45 minutes	This instrument provides a variety of subtests that explore receptive, expressive, and pragmatic language
				Students mostly need to provide responses (rather than choose the right answer) which helps to identify challenges in social problem solving

cont.

Name	Publisher	Age	Time	Description
The Listening Comprehension Test-2 (LCT-2)	Huisingh, Bowers, and LoGiudice, 2006	6–11	35–40 minutes	This test consists of five subtests that all require open-ended responses The subtests probe: Main idea, Detail, Reasoning, Vocabulary, and Understanding Messages Many clinicians have found this tool useful in learning about a student's strengths and weaknesses
Test of Language Competence (TLC-Expanded)	Wiig and Secord, 1989	Level 1:5–9 Level 2:10–18	Less than 60 minutes	This test consists of subtests which explore the more abstract elements of receptive and expressive language including: 1) Ambiguous Sentences, 2) Listening Comprehension, 3) Oral Expression-Recreating Speech Acts, 4) Figurative Language, and 5) Supplemental Memory

GLOBAL SOCIAL FUNCTIONING: OBSERVATION

Beyond standardized assessments of global functioning and language assessments, it is important to know what the student is actually doing or not doing in the social environment. It is particularly helpful for the team to get a sense of how the student with social challenges functions on the playground or in the cafeteria compared with his peers. Peer interactions are critical for determining skills and challenges. For example, a student with ASD who has received structured interventions for many years from a variety of adult therapists might manage well around adults. These adults learn to compensate and support the student with social challenges. However, the student's social skills may still be very shaky with peers who usually don't modify their behavior. Thus, a student who has learned to interact with sympathetic adults may still struggle with peers. These social challenges become clear in a natural setting like the cafeteria or playground.

The best way to collect this information is through direct, unstructured observation of the student in the natural environments. The word, "unstructured" implies that the student is not asked to do anything during the observation. The observer is merely observing the student's behavior with peers. However, the information should be carefully collected so the result is documented evidence of challenges that need intervention. Below are some examples of strategies and scales that can be used to document evidence of challenges observed in natural settings. The Observation Recording Form is found in Appendix IV.

Super Skills Profile of Social Difficulty (SSPSD)

The SSPSD (Coucouvanis, 2005) is based on careful observation of a student across multiple settings. It can identify a precise target for intervention and may even inform an IEP. Plan on using this assessment to establish baseline skills, and administer it periodically throughout the school year to identify improvement in targeted areas as well as possible collateral social gains. Changes over time can be graphed to track progress. The SSPSD is found in Appendix IV.

Direct interview

In addition to direct observation, reports from other people who have opportunities to observe the student's social functioning can be an asset to FRIEND®. An observation can reveal the functional impairment but not explain what causes the impairment in the first place. To understand the impairment and its cause, an interview can be a powerful complement to observation. The FRIEND team needs to identify challenges to establishing and maintaining relationships. The challenges will differ according to each individual student. Not all students with challenges need the same intervention strategies, and not all students will benefit from learning the same skills. For example, some students with social challenges never begin conversations, while others ask questions non-stop. Some avoid their peers completely, while others routinely invade personal space. Some students may not know how to engage, while others may talk endlessly about Disney princesses, batteries, or the weather. All these scenarios, while qualitatively different, will lead to social challenges that can be addressed in FRIEND®. A combination of observations and interviews is the best way to identify the function of the impairment.

The Social Functioning Interview (SFI)

Ideally, the SFI (adapted from *Building Social Relationships*; Bellini, 2006a and found in Appendix III) is conducted with a student's teacher, parents, and whenever possible, the student him- or herself. The combined information provides a profile of the student that includes a summary of social functioning, communication, and interests across multiple settings. From this summary, the team may better understand the function of the impairment and address it appropriately with intervention.

Information from teachers can add a valuable perspective to the SFI. Not only do they observe the student with social challenges, but they have the unique opportunity to observe the social functioning of 25 students for a full school year, and do this year after year. Because of this experience, they may be the best professionals to identify difference from the norm. Rarely are parents or other professionals privy to such information regarding social functioning, nor do they have the opportunity to develop such expertise through exposure.

Parents also add a valuable but different perspective to the SFI. A student is often most comfortable in the home and this may be where his or her true personality emerges. It is important to gather data on social opportunities in the community and at home when the student is with his or her family. This approach also allows members of the team to include parents and family members in the FRIEND process.

Involving students in the SFI can enrich the team's understanding of an individual's particular challenges and the individual's understanding of those challenges. The self-report may uncover social opportunities unknown to the team. It is important to consider the following when collecting information from students with self-report measures:

- Ensure that the measure is appropriate for the cognitive level of the student.

- Make sure that the student understands the questions.

- Encourage the student to ask questions.

- Compare the student's ratings with those of parents and teachers.

- Let the information from the student guide additional probes.

While direct interviews provide an opportunity for the more experienced personnel to explore relevant topics in a conversation with the respondent in such a way that can improve the accuracy of the information collected, they are also time consuming. If time and resources do not allow for a direct interview, rather than lose the information entirely we recommend using the SFI forms as questionnaires. Staff can always follow up on information they believe to be relevant.

FRIEND®: GOALS, INTERVENTIONS, AND OBJECTIVES

Once general information is collected through observation, the information can structure the intervention plan. A well-formed intervention plan includes goals and objectives. Goals are general skill areas while objectives are activities the student works toward and eventually masters. Objectives should be SMART: specific, measurable, achievable, realistic, and time-related (Doran, 1981). Objectives become the unit of measurement to help determine the effectiveness of the intervention. All three components (goals, interventions, and objectives) work together to help the student develop skills necessary to reach a sample goal of "appropriate interaction with peers 80 percent of the time at lunch," which in turn leads to improved functioning and overall quality of life.

An objective that might help the student reach the goal is to gain knowledge of age-appropriate games or topics because with this kind of information he or she can better relate to peers. The team should decide to implement intervention, or activities, that will develop this kind of knowledge. An intervention might be to start watching a popular television show and discussing it with the family. This activity will help the student reach the objective "gaining knowledge about peer interests" of the intervention.

At the center of this relationship are skills. All three components of FRIEND® are essentially building the student's social and communication skills. Each objective relates to a specific skill, and goals require a collection of skills to be attained. An effective FRIEND program builds skills, and measuring skills (achieved through interventions and objectives) helps determine progress and success.

Figure 4.1 demonstrates the relationship between a goal, objectives, interventions, and skills. It is necessary for the FRIEND team to think in one direction, while the processes for the student happen in the opposite direction. That is, the team decides on the goals to help improve quality of life for the student, then breaks each goal into smaller objectives and decides on interventions that will help build the required skills. The student, through intervention, will first build the skills, then meet the objectives and ultimately a goal. This same model can be followed for each goal in a student's program. The objectives for a particular goal will vary, but all objectives should be realistic, measurable, and meaningful. For example, if a student with ASD was engaged with peers for 10 percent of the recess period at baseline, it would be unrealistic to establish a goal of 80 percent during recess after three months. A more reasonable goal may be to increase engagement from 10 percent to 30 percent. Each student's goals and objectives should be based on his or her skills at baseline.

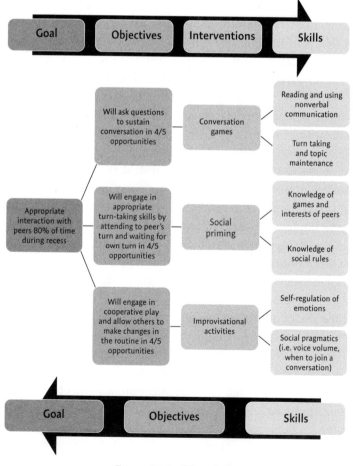

Figure 4.1 Building skills

Another example of how goals, skills, interventions, and objectives interact is included in Table 4.4. This example does not include all the possible skills, interventions, and objectives appropriate for a particular student. Remember, objectives differ depending upon a student's baseline skills.

Table 4.4 An example of goal/objectives/interventions/skills interaction

Goal
Student will interact with peers appropriately 80 percent of the time at recess and lunch
Objectives
To reach this goal, the student will: • increase duration of engagement in large group activities to 50 percent • require fewer prompts to engage in activities (specific number of prompts will depend on baseline assessment) • increase cooperative play with peers to 70 percent of structured activities • demonstrate an increase in the number of conversational exchanges with a typical peer/adult from one to three (conversational turn taking) during a 30-minute recess • eat lunch with typical peers, and engage in a minimum of four developmentally appropriate communicative exchanges independently, at least four of five days each week • increase age-appropriate waiting and turn taking to 50 percent of opportunities • communicate with adult/peers appropriately when peer does not follow the rules—70 percent of opportunities • increase flexibility at recess to include three different play activities • comply with peer directions 70 percent of opportunities • respond appropriately to social initiations from peers 50 percent of opportunities • request a preferred item and/or activity from an adult or peer three times during recess

cont.

Interventions

To complete these objectives, the FRIEND® team will use the following strategies:

- conversation games
- role playing
- improvisational activities
- teaching social rules
- Social Stories™
- social priming
- self-monitoring
- self-management

Skills

As a result, the student will develop skills in the following areas:

- reading nonverbal and contextual cues
- knowledge of social rules
- self-regulation of emotions
- knowledge of games and interests of peers
- use of nonverbal communication, including eye contact
- turn taking
- timing of responses
- social pragmatics (i.e. voice volume, when to join a conversation)
- topic maintenance
- theory of mind (perspective taking)

GOAL DEVELOPMENT

Well-defined, measurable goals are critical to the success of FRIEND®. A goal is a measurable component of a student's social functioning that improves quality of life. Goals are what FRIEND is working toward. The goal from our example, "to appropriately interact with peers during 80 percent of the time at lunch," is measurable because the interactions that occur during lunch can be observed and quantified. If goals are too broad or too general, like "develop social competence," they can be too difficult to measure and the team will have a hard time determining if the program is effective.

The assessment process described earlier in this chapter reveals the student's challenges and his or her strengths and interests. Figure 4.2 illustrates how the assessment process leads to meaningful planning.

Goals are important for the following reasons:

- Goals create a meaningful, individualized link between a student's assessments and the intervention strategies created for him or her.

- Goals represent clarity and agreement about the team's intentions. Everyone is on the same page.

- Goals represent objectivity and accountability.

- Goals use the team's expertise to establish functional social objectives.

- Goals help the team know when it has reached success by accomplishing the desired outcome.

Figure 4.2 The FRIEND® assessment process

It is important to set realistic expectations for the program, the team, and, perhaps most importantly, the student. Some students' challenges may indicate that only one or two goals can have a significant impact, while other students' challenges may require more goals. We recommend designing a program to achieve no more than three goals in a given time period, but that time period can vary from student to student. Just be careful not to overburden the FRIEND® team because it will surely lead to diminished effectiveness and support for the program and the student.

Breaking goals down into objectives

Goals are big changes and may take longer to achieve, so recognizing the smaller parts of each goal will help make the program more manageable. Objectives become the map and compass for FRIEND® to build skills. They add structure to the program. With objectives, FRIEND can navigate with a clear destination in mind. Objectives are the everyday behaviors for the student with social challenges to practice. While the goal of FRIEND is to build social skills, the daily objectives improve the quality of life for students with social challenges because they can engage in more satisfying social interactions.

Interventions

Interventions are the activities the FRIEND team creates to engage the student with social challenges and the typical peers in the program. It is critical to the success of the intervention that activities be interesting and motivating. Interventions are designed to actively teach and practice skills. As skills are developed in the student, objectives are reached.

It is important to differentiate activities from objectives. An objective might be to increase the duration of time spent in large group activities. An intervention would create opportunities for the student to practice skills needed for group activities. For example, the group might play a board game that involves turn taking and friendly conversation, or they might have a pizza party lunch where all students discuss a favorite television show. It is important not to confuse the objective with the intervention. That is, a facilitator should never say, "go play that game with those students over there and stay for 10 minutes this time." The idea is for the student to be motivated to maintain engagement and develop the skills to be successful.

Social priming is an intervention to help students learn and practice ways to engage with peers socially. An objective of social priming might be to engage with peers in four appropriate conversational exchanges. It would be difficult for a student with social challenges to have a meaningful conversation about a popular cartoon if he or she had no experience doing so. In social priming, parents can create opportunities to watch and discuss the cartoon at home over dinner, and the student can then practice the skill at school (during lunch) and meet the objective. Interventions and objectives work together to build the skills needed to reach the goal.

FRIEND® favors an intervention approach consistent with the principles of applied behavior analysis. That is, effective intervention strategies should always have clear and measurable objectives. Data is collected on the number of opportunities presented and when the student is successful. Progress can be measured and data can help inform the team of success or areas that need improvement. There are many different intervention strategies aligned with this approach designed to improve social skills. The flexibility of FRIEND allows the team to include any intervention strategy as long as opportunities are provided to the student to practice appropriate or desired behavior. Specific intervention strategies are discussed in more detail in Chapters 6 and 7.

BASELINE DATA COLLECTION

Before you can make progress, you have to know how to measure progress. Effective intervention programs start with baseline data collection on current skills. Baseline data helps ensure the student is making measurable progress. If the student is not making progress, then something in the program needs to be adjusted.

Consistency in measurement methods is important to make sure the team is comparing apples with apples. The assessments you conduct at baseline should be repeated throughout the program. If you begin to use a new assessment part way through, there will be no data to compare it against that will allow you to measure progress. Choose your baseline assessments carefully.

Ideally, data should be collected by an objective staff member at the school who is not directly involved in the intervention. The data collector should have some experience with observing and coding relevant aspects of behavior. For example, the person should know what a social initiation looks like, and be able to gauge the appropriate qualities of such attempts. Baseline data should be reviewed prior to collecting follow-up data. Data should not be collected while the program is being implemented to obtain a clear, unbiased measure of the student's spontaneous functioning.

Observation of social functioning

Although there are many social goals which may emerge from your team's assessment, the following four measures are often a good place to begin. Definitions of each skill are provided later in this chapter:

1. number of social initiations to peers (from the student)

2. engagement in an activity with peers (duration of time)

3. number of social initiations from peers (to the student)

4. social responses to peers (frequency).

We recommend collecting baseline data for five to ten minutes on three separate days in different settings to provide an accurate picture of a student's functioning. Data should be taken for each social and communication goal written for the student. The most challenging social times of the day are periods of unstructured social activity. Therefore, the ideal times to collect baseline data are:

- on the playground

- during lunch

- during a less structured period of the school day (e.g. during a collaborative classroom project).

Observing the student during unstructured times of the school day reveals behavior that is authentic and spontaneous. We suggest these different settings because they allow the team to see the student's functioning with different peers and may reveal consistencies (or inconsistencies) that are clinically relevant. The team may learn what makes social behavior easier or more challenging for the student. Observations in natural settings can also help the team learn about typical behavior as well, which can be an important benchmark. That is, observers can collect data on typical peers too, and set goals for the student with social challenges.

The Observation Recording Form

Data should always be collected in an organized and uniform method. If there are two observers collecting data in different settings, they need to be consistent. Raters should have clear definitions of the target behaviors they are observing. The Observation Recording Form in Appendix IV provides definitions, method of recording, and space to record observations across multiple settings and days. It will add the organization and consistency needed for the program.

The form includes five different behaviors to be assessed, which are defined in the form. These behaviors should provide a comprehensive assessment of the student's functioning in the naturalistic setting. Note that one of the behaviors measured is social initiation by a peer. While this behavior is not an objective for the target student, it does reflect how successfully FRIEND® supports peers as they increase their competence and confidence in interacting with their socially challenged classmates.

The recording form also provides space for you to make notes on your general observations of factors that can affect behavior and have an impact on the intervention. Some examples of these factors are listed in Table 4.5.

Table 4.5 General observations form

Interests of the student
• Activities
• Peers
Physical characteristics of the environment
• Noise level
• Sensory distracters
• Sensory seeking behavior
Motor planning challenges
• Gross motor
• Fine motor
Social pragmatics
• Eye contact
• Volume/tone of speech
• Responsiveness

MONITORING PROGRESS

Eight-year-old Pui initiated many conversations with peers about dinosaurs and aquatic animals, but failed to respond appropriately when a classmate made a comment or asked a question about a different topic. He had been in FRIEND for approximately three months and it was time to see if he was making progress. In this program, data was collected every week recording the percentage of times Pui appropriately responded to a classmate about a non-preferred topic. Pui went from 20 percent at baseline to 90 percent after three months of intervention. At the end of that three-month period, the assessment was repeated to determine possible collateral social skill improvement as well as other areas of needed improvement. Through regular data collection that occurs during FRIEND® and the follow-up assessments after three months, it was clear that Pui was making progress, but he still needed support. Now the team had a clear idea of what to target next.

Observational data should be taken on a consistent predetermined schedule to measure the student's progress. Data may be collected daily for an intensive intervention, twice weekly to ensure that facilitators and peers are oriented and comfortable in their roles, and eventually weekly once interventions are implemented and fine-tuned. Frequent data collection will allow for effective monitoring of the intervention and will help the FRIEND team determine when modifications are needed.

We recommend that global skills assessments (like the observation of social functioning described above) be conducted every three months, but the time period can be adjusted to meet the needs of the student with social challenges and the FRIEND team. It is best initially to err on the side of conducting assessments more frequently so you can determine if adjustments need to be made before too much time has passed. Over time, the team will develop knowledge that pertains to the individual student and can adjust the schedule as necessary.

EVALUATING DATA

Graphing data is a way to quickly and easily determine if progress is being made, and at what rate the progress is occurring. Observational data should be reviewed as needed and the intervention team should meet quarterly to evaluate the data. Figure 4.3 shows progress based on data collected daily regarding a student's conversations with peers. From the graph we can see the improvements in appropriate statements and the decline in inappropriate statements, indicating the student is making progress.

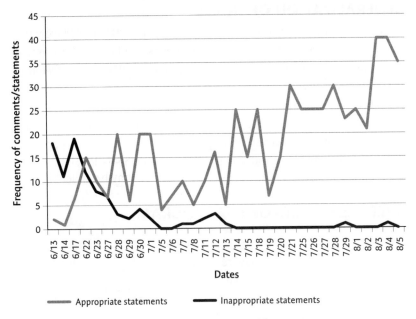

Figure 4.3 Conversations with peers

MAKING DATA-BASED DECISIONS

For some behaviors, such as time engaged with peers, improvement may be seen immediately after implementing FRIEND®. For other behaviors progress may take longer. It is important for the team to understand the differences in such skills and gauge expectations appropriately. For a behavior such as spontaneous initiations many factors come into play. The student needs to learn a lot about the peers and their interests, practice other skills frequently, and build confidence to make an approach. This kind of skill takes a reasonable amount of time. Since all students learn and interact differently, time allotments cannot be suggested, but should be determined by the group that knows the student best and understands the environment. Making changes too soon can be just as much of a time waster as sticking with an ineffective program for too long.

GENERALIZATION OF SKILLS

Once a social or communication goal has been met on the playground or in the lunchroom, it is important to measure that same behavior in other environments. By measuring social interactions during free time or transitions between classes, the team can evaluate the generalization of skills across settings. Before determining if a goal has been mastered, check to see that the behavior has generalized to other environments and is being exhibited with a variety of peers. Conversations with parents at IEP meetings may be a good way to collect this information.

OVERALL EFFECTS OF THE PROGRAM

Whether it is the unstructured environment, the lack of friends, or the inability to initiate play, recess can create feelings of fear and inadequacy for children with social challenges. As the assistant principal for a public K-5 school in charge of discipline, I have tracked the high number of office referrals during recess versus other activities during school.

Since the implementation of FRIEND® there has been a significant decrease in the number of office referrals for playground misbehavior. This can be traced, in my opinion, to the fact that there is more structure on the playground. I have also seen kinder behavior from the typical students toward each other and toward the students with social challenges. There has been a dramatic improvement in the students with special needs' ability to initiate and participate in social activities. FRIEND has been a win-win situation for all of our students.

Measures such as number of office referrals or frequency of disciplinary actions by playground and lunchroom monitors can be used to measure overall effects of FRIEND. Other measures can be taken such as number of students not appropriately engaged at recess or number of students sitting alone at lunch to determine if the program has an effect on behavior of all students, not just the target students in the program. Before starting FRIEND at a school, it would be helpful to collect and record these baseline data points to help measure and document collateral gains.

SOCIAL VALIDITY AND FIDELITY

FRIEND® involves a team effort, which consists of parents, peer participants, teachers, therapists, cafeteria workers, educational aides, and the
student him- or herself. Each member of the team serves a critical role
in the success of FRIEND; each team member must take ownership and
responsibility for the program. It is essential to give each team member
the opportunity to think about the program from their point of view, and
give feedback on a regular basis.

Social validity

This is a concept that captures how strongly the team members believe
that what they are doing will make a real difference. That is, if the school
and those expected to administer FRIEND believe in the program, they
will do their best to do it correctly (Gresham and Lambros, 1998). If
school administrators and staff do not understand FRIEND, or do not
believe that it will useful to the student with social challenges, they are
less likely to implement the program with fidelity.

Forms provided in Appendix VI give FRIEND team members the
opportunity to rate the social validity of the program. Most schools only
measure social validity one time, either at the beginning or shortly after
FRIEND has begun. If social validity is less than expected, additional
training for the staff may help to change their thoughts about the program.
If so, then social validity should be measured again before going forward
with the program.

Treatment fidelity

This refers to the degree that intervention strategies are being implemented as intended. This is essential to the success of the program.
Measuring treatment fidelity can determine current training needs of staff
implementing the program and can also be used to analyze data related
to student goals. If the student is not making progress, it's important to
determine if the program is implemented correctly or if the program is
not successful at targeting a particular goal.

If the program is not being implemented with fidelity, it is important
to assess the reasons. These may include poor staff training, inadequate
supervision, time constraints, or a lack of staff and administrative support.

Treatment fidelity can be measured by directly observing whether the strategies are implemented properly on a given day. A tool to measure fidelity of implementation of the FRIEND® lunch and playground programs can also be found in Appendix VI.

CHAPTER SUMMARY

✓ There are multiple options for standardized assessment of various challenges for socialization and communication. Questionnaires are good for measuring specific deficits but may not tell you about the cause of the deficit. Direct observation of the student's functioning over time may help to fill in the gaps.

✓ The student's present level of social functioning is continually monitored and compared with past levels of performance to document progress as a result of a particular intervention. Social performance should be measured at the beginning of FRIEND and as needed. Ideally, a direct observation of social performance should be made weekly throughout the school year.

✓ Interviews with parents and education professionals provide feedback on their perception of the student's progress. These interviews provide information on the appropriateness of the objectives and the strategies currently being implemented.

✓ Monitoring progress of FRIEND® involves collecting data on social functioning, communication, and plays skills through observations, interviews, and standardized rating scales.

✓ Three elements to add structure to FRIEND are goals, objectives, and interventions. The team identifies goals for a student and then develops daily objectives for the student. The interventions are the activities that help the student meet the objectives. Through interventions, the student begins to meet daily objectives and builds skills that will ultimately meet a goal.

✓ Social validity is a concept that captures how strongly the team members believe that what they are doing will make a real difference. Treatment fidelity refers to the degree to which FRIEND is implemented as intended.

5

The Peer Sensitivity Program

In a peer sensitivity program for a socially challenged third grader, I asked students to break up into small groups without any direction from me. I wanted to see what would happen. I noticed the student with ASD and two others were not included in any group. They stood alone, waiting. I watched these students and waited, hoping the teachers would notice and help them join a group. Neither the adults nor the students showed any understanding or awareness that their classmates were clearly left out.

INTRODUCTION

As schools move toward best practices of inclusion almost every classroom will have students who need some kind of social support. Fortunately, strategies associated with FRIEND® benefit all students by encouraging acceptance, tolerance, and opportunities to learn new skills.

Environments that embrace PBS, anti-bullying campaigns, and other school-wide policies (e.g. "no child sits alone") are on the right track. While good general strategies, these programs do not train staff and students about the specific behaviors associated with a student's challenges. All students are different and so are their challenges. Therefore, student-specific peer sensitivity training will likely be more effective than school-wide programs.

An effective peer sensitivity program (PSP) will provide training not only to students but to staff as well. All who observe differences in a student with social challenges can benefit from training to:

- better understand the differences he or she sees

- respond appropriately to differences

- encourage the student to engage in appropriate social behavior.

Tips for students and staff can be found in Appendix V.

Peer and adult support play critical roles in decreasing the likelihood that a student with ASD will develop social anxiety (Bellini, 2006a). Improving peer sensitivity can help create a supportive social environment for all students with challenges to develop better social skills.

At times, each and every student will display behaviors that make them seem different or odd to other students. If these behaviors are infrequent or not dramatically deviant, they may not present difficulties to developing social relationships. When odd behaviors are frequent and regular, other students notice. If the students accept what they see and take it in stride, there is no real problem to address. However, when students observe odd behaviors and comment, or act on what they see by shunning or teasing the student, they need help to understand what they see and act appropriately. Baker (2003) recommends that student-specific disability training is held when a student displays regularly observable behaviors that are commented on by other students.

> When Luke's teachers suggested we present a peer sensitivity training to his fourth grade class they asked us if we wanted to mention his diagnosis. Our primary concern was what would be best for Luke. Luke had many self-stimulatory behaviors like pacing on the playground. He was not conversational with other students and did not know how to play during recess.
>
> We felt as a family it was best for other students to know that Luke had autism. It seemed that every week there was a news special, movie, TV show, or public service announcement about autism. So, it seemed only appropriate to use the word autism when teaching other students how to help and support him. We felt that as services for kids with autism improved over time, it would be in part because there was clarity and consensus about how to help Luke and other kids like him.

If a student's social challenges are part of a diagnosed disorder, then the issue of disclosure, to the class or even the student, needs to be discussed with the parents and the FRIEND® team. Some parents may not have disclosed the diagnosis to the student. As a result, they may express some ambivalence about the need for a PSP. To disclose or not to disclose, how to disclose, and how much to disclose is a family decision and every family is different. If the parents have decided against disclosing, a PSP is still beneficial. The discussion in this context may be the impetus for the parents to disclose the diagnosis to their child.

> I was pleased when Jennifer's parents approached me about providing a peer sensitivity presentation for her class. As her teacher I'd often heard Jennifer's classmates talking about her behaviors which were typical of Asperger's Syndrome. As we prepared for this presentation Jennifer's parents disclosed that they had never discussed the diagnosis with their daughter. I raised the concern that everyone else would know about Jennifer's diagnosis except Jennifer. Jennifer knew she was different and often wrote about this in her journal, but she never knew her diagnosis. Her parents realized that they needed to talk with Jennifer first and allow her to process the information before we implemented the PSP to her class.

Some parents may prefer not to use the terms autism, Asperger's, ASD, or any other disability-specific terminology. General terms, such as social/communication disorder or social differences, may be used. Parents may want to be involved in the peer sensitivity training, to share their child's interests and strengths with the group. The student's parents should always be aware of the content being presented in the peer sensitivity training.

TO DISCLOSE OR NOT TO DISCLOSE

Regardless of whether the diagnosis is disclosed to the student or the class, the student should be aware of what will be discussed during the PSP. Delegated school personnel will explain to the student that someone will be talking to their class about things they do well, and also about things they need help with, such as talking and playing. The depth of information to be disclosed is somewhat dependent upon the student's ability to understand the content. Only what is meaningful to the student should be disclosed. Too much information presented to the student with limited comprehension can be harmful or confusing.

> As a family we had decided to share Luke's diagnosis with him when he was eight. After he knew about his diagnosis we were able to talk about autism as a family. We learned together about how to help Luke overcome the challenges that came with the disorder. We told our extended family and neighbors that Luke had autism and how they could help him. The other kids in the neighborhood seemed to feel more comfortable around Luke once they knew that his occasional odd behavior was because he had autism, not because he was "weird."

> As the mother of a nine-year-old child with autism, Matt, I struggled with the decision of whether or not to share his diagnosis with his peers during a peer sensitivity training in his class. Matt was fully included in a general education classroom and was usually able to blend in well, but there were definite differences. When other kids wanted to play kickball or four-square, Matt preferred to look for bugs by himself. He spent a lot of time learning, talking about, and looking for bugs. It was painful to see him be alone so much. If I shared his diagnosis, the students might be more understanding, or they could exclude him even more. In the end, we decided as a family not to share Matt's diagnosis but went ahead with the training. FRIEND® helped Matt find a group of students to hang out with at lunch and recess. The program gave him opportunities to learn and practice appropriate social behaviors.

IMPLEMENTATION OF PEER SENSITIVITY TRAINING

Peer sensitivity training may produce positive changes in the behavior of students as they strive to be more tolerant, accepting, and helpful to each other. However, such discussions and/or activities may also lead to potentially hurtful situations if not presented with great care.

Set basic ground rules

When you have an open forum to discuss a specific student's differences, peers may feel it is a time to discuss all the behaviors they see the student exhibit. The group leader should be careful to avoid a free-for-all. Avoid the opportunity for students to call out things like, "He spins his hands when he walks around the playground," or "She only talks about Disney movies." If presented all at one time without structure, these comments could be hurtful. If comments are presented in a controlled environment with the expectation that everyone is learning better ways to communicate, the program will be more constructive.

Ground rules may be already established as part of the classroom, or additional rules may be developed specifically for this experience. Examples of basic ground rules may be:

- no name calling

- one speaker at a time

- raise your hand to speak

- listen when others speak

- if you don't have anything nice to say…

Know your group

- The most effective presentation will be geared to the students' developmental level. For younger children, make sure they understand the topic, and provide many examples so they can relate better to the discussion.

- In order to make the discussion relevant to the students, you may need to use analogies or references to things that interest them such as sports, video games, television shows, or favorite celebrities.

Make it comfortable

- Small group settings are better than larger auditoriums or lunchroom where there are distractions.

- Encourage participation from all students by setting the expectations early. Everyone should be prompted for comments.

- When selecting the time and place for the discussion, it is important to consider several factors that may interfere with students' ability to participate and attend to the discussion, including:

  – The length of the presentation: A presentation that is too short may not produce a lasting effect or the desired impact on the students' behavior. However, a presentation that is too long may become boring or quickly lose the interest of the students. Consider the amount of time your students can stay focused on a subject.

  – Presentation style:

    How do your students learn?

    Will one discussion be adequate for the students to understand the message?

    Do your students learn best with hands-on activities, visual props, a small discussion group, or a combination of these?

  – Frequency: It is unrealistic to expect big changes from only a small investment of time. When trying to change students' behavior, repetition and support will be most effective. Most anti-bullying programs are provided in auditoriums, to the whole school at once and for a short period of time and then school-wide changes in behavior are expected. For the PSP associated with FRIEND®, we recommend meeting with the class at least once per month, perhaps during lunch or a recess time. These time periods will not take time away from academics, and the frequency will allow for students to learn, practice, and be accountable for the behaviors toward the student with social challenges, and other students who need support. A bigger commitment to improving sensitivity will have bigger payoff.

GENERAL GUIDELINES

- **Listen to your students.** As the leader of the discussion, set the tone by listening to what your students have to say. Let your students express their concerns and make suggestions. By listening to them, you will better understand the stumbling blocks that may get in the way as they try to be helpful to others. When students feel that they are being listened to, they will be willing to try new things and listen to your suggestions.

- **There is no "bad comment."** Students should be encouraged to contribute to the discussion. If one student raises their hand to share an idea or ask a question that isn't appropriate to the discussion, kindly thank them for sharing. Try to use it appropriately in the discussion if possible.

- **Focus on the positive.** Generally, the focus of peer sensitivity training is to teach students about the challenges and difficulties people with ASD, a social challenge, or another disability may face. However, it is important for students to learn about the wonderful abilities that people with differences may have. Teach students to look for the positive things in others so they can appreciate them. This will help students build meaningful friendships based on mutual respect.

- **Use group experiences.** Group learning experiences are an excellent way for students to learn how to communicate, work with others, and solve conflicts. Dividing students into groups can be challenging. Many students have peers that they prefer to work with when given the opportunity. When asking students to self-select into groups, a few students are usually left without a group to join, which can be awkward, embarrassing, and very hurtful for the students who are left out. To avoid this situation, randomized group selection can be quick and easy. Some examples include:

  - Assign each student a number, up to the number of groups needed (e.g. 1–4 if four groups). Then establish a location for the ones to sit, the twos to sit, and so on…

  - Tear up strips of colored paper, one color for each group. Have each student pull a color from the bag and then join with the others of the same color. Variation: instead of colors, you can use categories, such as different food groups, animals, characters from the latest Disney movie or television shows, superheroes, and so on.

WHAT TO PRESENT

To help add structure to the PSP, the *I'm Here* activity guide produced by Fable Vision Learning can help make the presentation more focused and engaging. You can download it for free.[1]

I'm Here and the children's book *Wings of EPOH*, which has an accompanying DVD (Klein and Reynolds, 2008) are ideally suited for elementary age students.[2] The FRIEND® Activity Guide included in Appendix VII can provide guidance and suggestions for helpful group activities. In this manual, "Tips for Peers" (Appendix V) can be provided to students as a handout during the presentation. Discussion of these strategies may also help students understand ways they can support their peers.

If the parents and school personnel decided that it is best to disclose the student's diagnosis to the class, ensure that the information shared with other students is correct. Table 5.1, adapted from *Asperger's... What Does It Mean to Me?* by Catherine Faherty (2000), may be helpful for this purpose. The team may decide to use a part of this presentation, the entire presentation, or they can develop a new presentation, specific to the needs of the school or classroom.

Table 5.1 ASD presentation

ASD overview
• Highlight the strengths of all students in the class to create an opportunity to discuss the strengths of the student with ASD. It is important to highlight that strengths vary with the individual and are not always limited by the disorder.
• A student with ASD may be really good with reading and/or spelling but also may be good with foreign languages. Another student might be good at drawing and also mathematics and science. The point is everyone has their strengths and they may not always be obvious. Pointing out a student's hidden talents might start the road to acceptance.
• Autism is a pervasive developmental disorder. That is, people with autism develop more slowly than typically developing peers, and the difference is enough to impair their social and communication skills to the point where differences are obvious.
• Emphasize that people with ASD are very different from each other. Some children with ASD never talk, some talk a little, while some talk a lot. Clarify that the particular student with ASD known to these students will be different than other individuals with ASD, just as all of the students in the classroom are unique.

1   www.fablevisionlearning.com/im-here-activity-guide
2   www.shopbeneficialbeans.org/store/p172/Wings_of_Epoh_Book_%26_DVD_Bundle.html

- Point out that there are children and adults all over the world with autism. You may not know other students with ASD, but someday you might.

What is autism?

- While this definition may be clear to the person reading this manual, it may not be the best way to explain autism or ASD to students in elementary school. Furthermore, students in sixth grade will be able to understand more than students in kindergarten. Whatever language is used to explain the disorder, the core elements of ASD should be preserved. PSPs should explain that students with ASD:
  - have difficulty communicating
  - have difficulty socializing
  - display odd behaviors instead of playing the way other students do.

Common characteristics of children with ASD

Special interests

- Children with ASD may be very focused on their interests. It may be helpful to tell the class what a particular student's special interests are. Remind the class that just like each of them, the student with ASD may often talk about their interests.
- The student may want to play games at recess which focus on their special interests.
- Remind the student's classmates to tell the student with ASD what they are interested in too, which will encourage conversation and friendship.

Styles of learning

- Everyone learns in a different way. Some children with ASD learn better by looking at pictures or reading instead of listening to lectures. Or, they may learn better if the topic is related to their interests.
- Remind the student's peers to invite them to try something new at recess; they'll learn faster if their peers tell them and show them what to do.

Routines and familiarity

- Students with ASD may like routines and familiarity.
- Routines may help students with ASD feel comfortable, because routines help students know what is going to happen and when it is going to happen.
- A student with ASD may use a visual schedule to know what will happen next.
- The student's peers can help their classmate with ASD by telling them what to expect next.

cont.

Common characteristics of children with ASD

Movements

- Many children with ASD move their bodies in particular ways. They may move their hands, wiggle their fingers, jump up and down, rock back and forth, spin around, or pace back and forth.

- Peers can help students with ASD play more typically on the playground. If they see a student making odd movements by themselves, they can invite the student to go on the swings, go down the slide, or play games with other typical students.

Communication

- Communication might not always be easy, natural, or fun for students with ASD.

- Every student can learn to be a better communicator.

- Each of the students in the classroom can have many opportunities to practice talking with the student with ASD about interesting things.

The five senses

- Many students with ASD experience their senses differently than their peers who do not have ASD.

- Sometimes what a student with ASD experiences through their senses feels good, but sometimes it may feel uncomfortable, painful, or overwhelming.

Hearing

- Some students with ASD are bothered by sudden noises, like fire alarms.

- The teacher may help prepare a student with ASD for a fire alarm. He or she may tell him or her when it will occur. The student's peers can show them where to go and remind them to put their hands over their ears if that helps them be more comfortable.

- Some students with ASD notice quiet sounds that other classmates don't notice, like: birds and insects, fluorescent lights, fans, computers, people talking or working in other rooms, people breathing, or people turning pages in books nearby.

- Peers can kindly remind the student with ASD to pay attention to what the teacher is saying, or what he or she needs to do next, if they are distracted by quiet classroom noises.

Touch

- Sometimes touch feels comfortable, but sometimes it may bother students with ASD.

- Peers should avoid rough play or uninvited hugs with a student with ASD if they seem uncomfortable with those experiences.

Smell
- Many children with ASD pay attention to how things smell. They may especially like some smells, but can be bothered by others. This might make it hard to concentrate.
- Peers may observe the student with ASD seeking out certain smells. If the student with ASD is distracted by smells, they may need to be reminded to pay attention in class.

Sight
- Many students with ASD see things other people do not notice.
- Some students with ASD really like to watch or look at certain things.
- Some students with ASD get confused or anxious when there are too many things to see at the same time.
- Encourage peers to be patient if their classmate with ASD doesn't automatically know what they should be looking at.
- Suggest that peers try to make eye contact with the student with ASD when talking with them or interacting with them.

Taste
- Peers should be encouraged to be patient with their classmate with ASD at lunch. With parent permission, the PSP can include a discussion about sharing foods. Parents can pack extra food for the student to bring to school and share with peers. Peers can also offer the student with ASD a new food.
- Students with ASD are more likely to try a new food that is similar to a familiar food. For example, if a student with ASD likes a certain kind of cracker, they are more likely to try and like a similar cracker if a peer offers it to them.

Adapted from Faherty (2000)

AFTER THE TRAINING
Challenge the students

To end the training, challenge the students to apply what they've learned. This will make the training applicable, and will let the students know that this is a real expectation. The results of the challenges can be discussed at the next session. Good suggestions for challenge activities can be found in the FRIEND® Activity Guide in Appendix VII. Some challenge examples are:

- Give them an assignment to learn more about another student over the next week and write about their experiences.
- Use an incentive program for the class. Every time the aide or teacher sees any student being kind, supportive, or helpful to

another person, they can put a sticker on a poster or chart. Once there are a pre-determined number of stickers (50–100) on the poster, the class will be rewarded as appropriate (homework passes, popcorn or pizza party, or other meaningful reward). This is a great way to encourage a supportive class culture as the students work together.

- Review the "Tips for Peers" handout (Appendix V) and encourage the students to take the handout home to their parents. This gives the students opportunities to talk about the many ways they can be supportive to a classmate with ASD. Parents' awareness of FRIEND® will increase the likelihood that students with ASD will be included in both neighborhood and community activities.

Identify a contact person

Learning to help a child with ASD, or other disability, can be challenging and difficult for typical peers. It is important to conclude the training by identifying a contact person who the students can go to with any questions or concerns. The contact person can be the teacher, aide, speech therapist, or anyone accessible to the students. Make it clear to the students that it is appropriate to have questions or concerns after the training. A contact person who is familiar with the student with ASD should be designated to respond to peers' questions or comments.

Follow up

Once the training is complete, the students may remember their experiences and follow through with any assignments or commitments made for the first few weeks. However, over time, the experience may be forgotten and students could forget the challenge.

A study of a similar program found that immediately following a class discussion, acceptance scores of the focus child (the child with a disability) initially increased while rejection scores decreased. However, over an 18-week period of time, the acceptance and rejection scores returned to baseline (Frederickson, Warren, and Turner, 2005).

To maintain a positive change from peer sensitivity, we recommend the class meet on a monthly basis. Frequency of meetings will improve the likelihood that your PSP will be effective and promote positive behavioral change.

CHAPTER SUMMARY

✓ An important aspect of FRIEND® is to provide the student's classmates (and teachers) with a basic understanding of the disorder. While peer sensitivity trainings are designed to help a specific student, there are many additional benefits of such discussions in the classroom.

✓ Through guided experience and discussion, students may learn the benefits of collaboration, identification of other people's strengths, and conflict resolution. They may also gain a deeper understanding of the importance of not only accepting, but being kind and helpful to others.

✓ Strategies for a successful peer sensitivity presentation include: select an educator and/or parent knowledgeable about ASD who will present to the class, know your group, make it comfortable, set ground rules, use appropriate and engaging resources to explain ASD, listen to your students, remember that there is no "bad comment," focus on the positive, highlight group experiences, challenge the students, identify a contact person, and follow up.

✓ Classmates who participate in PSPs report personal growth, greater understanding of self, improved attitudes toward people with disabilities, greater appreciation of diversity, new advocacy skills, and lasting friendships.

✓ A PSP can positively impact the culture of the school and the surrounding community, but only if appropriate time and effort is invested in changing the behavior of all students. A PSP should include structured meetings with students in small groups on a regular schedule throughout the school year.

6

The FRIEND®
Lunch Program

When my son, Harry, started middle school I knew he would be sitting alone during lunch, surrounded by peers talking and having fun with each other. I wanted more for Harry. I wanted him to have friends who supported him, and a better quality of life than he was able to create on his own. Our intervention approach was always based on inclusion, but that was mainly in the classroom. I wanted a structured inclusion for lunchtime as well, so I worked with the school to start the FLP.

To find peers who were interested, we distributed a flyer that referred to a lunchtime group and I offered pizza. Thirty students came to the first meeting. I was thrilled, but Harry was overwhelmed. There was little structure, the students didn't know how to support Harry, and we ran out of pizza. We needed to plan better. Eventually we identified three boys that were already friends with each other. They knew Harry and shared the same interests. They were excited about being part of a lunch program that included games and pizza every two weeks.

Over the next three years these boys continued in the FLP. Of course, there were challenges. Sometimes the kids were more interested in talking to each other than with Harry, but they got the feedback and support they needed to make the program successful. Plus, they had fun and liked the pizza. Today, Harry is 23, and he still has his challenges, but he loves to engage socially with peers. What he learned in FRIEND® went a long way.

INTRODUCTION

Lunchtime can be challenging for any student dealing with the noise and chaos associated with hungry students set free for a brief time from the shackles of the classroom. Kids are loud and rambunctious as they hurry to eat, socialize, and get in some play before lunchtime is over. Navigation through all of that takes expertise that is easily taken for granted. Most kids do all of it effortlessly. However, the non-expert—the student with social challenges—struggles, often not getting anything positive from any interaction.

The FLP provides structure and peer support among the chaos. It can take place in the cafeteria, at outside lunch tables, or maybe in an empty classroom. In this part of FRIEND®, the Lunch Group is formed early in the process. It usually includes one or two students with challenges and a few committed peers. The peers are essential because they facilitate appropriate interactions and support the student with challenges. As with any intervention program, frequency is directly related to outcomes. The more the intervention occurs, the more opportunities for learning, and the more skills will be developed. Ideally, the FRIEND Lunch Group will meet daily throughout the school year. If this is not possible for any reason, then the best advice is for them to meet as frequently as possible, at least several times each week.

Training and support from school personnel for the FRIEND Lunch Group will be minimal but necessary. We recommend an initial orientation and periodic follow-up meetings for students to discuss how things are going, problem solve, and make suggestions about how to make lunchtime discussions more effective and the group more cohesive. The meetings should be fun, may include games and food, but most importantly they should be supportive and provide specific feedback and suggestions.

FRIEND is about inclusion in typical environments, not exclusion, so the FRIEND Lunch Group should look like a group of students having lunch together, and care should be taken to avoid having the group look different. Observation of lunchtime behavior will be necessary because staff need to see how typical students behave and what they talk about. With this information it will be easier to create a more effective lunch program that will benefit all participants.

Ideally, all students in the FRIEND Lunch Group will continue to participate throughout the school year, or even for multiple years. If a student decides they no longer want to participate, the program shouldn't end. Groups of typically developing students evolve and change over time and so can the Lunch Group. Instead of ending, another student who is interested, preferably a friend of someone already in the group, can be asked to join at any time. Keep in mind though that the program will be less effective if the peers are substituted regularly, or if they don't want to be there. Students should want to be a part of the group. Members of the group should be consistent so the student with challenges (and really all the students in the group) can develop relationships with each other.

THE FLP IMPLEMENTATION
Planning

The FLP will be most effective when it is well supported by the school. The more people invested in the program, the more likely it will succeed. Helpful planning documents can be found in Appendix II. As with any program, some advanced planning goes a long way toward successful implementation. Of course, it is ideal if all aspects of FRIEND® (the PSP, Lunch Program, and Playground Program) are planned and staffed at the same time. This ensures continuity, the sharing of ideas, strategies, and data, and consistency of interventions across settings. FRIEND may be initiated by a motivated educator or parent but effective implementation requires collaboration. Table 6.1 illustrates how planning for the PSP and the FRIEND Lunch and Playground Programs can be integrated at the IEP and ongoing planning meetings.

Table 6.1 The FLP levels of support

Group	Frequency	Reason

IEP (IEP team members)	Once or twice a year	• Introduce FRIEND program in context of a particular student's social challenges
		• Determine assessment tools and who will collect data on playground and at lunch
		• PSP?
		  – Educators and parents collaborate on content
		  – Who will present?

cont.

Group	Frequency	Reason
Planning team (parents and school staff)	Monthly, bi-monthly or quarterly (as needed)	• Determine staffing: FRIEND® lunch/playground supervisors and facilitators; roles may overlap • Review baseline data • Determine social, communication, and play goals and objectives and data collection tools for lunch/playground • Update goals/objectives and interventions as skills emerge • Share strategies between parents and educators so that interventions are extended to home and community
Peers (peer participants supervisor)	Monthly (as needed)	**Provide ongoing training and support** • Review roles and intervention strategies • Answer questions in a confidential setting
Student with social challenges and supervisor	Monthly (as needed)	• Review program goals • Answer questions in a confidential setting
FRIEND Lunch Group check-in meeting (student with social challenges, peers, supervisor, and facilitator)	Weekly, bi-weekly or monthly (as needed)	**Build cohesiveness, cooperation, and commitment among all participants** • Answer questions, model strategies • Play fun, language-based games
Daily FRIEND Lunch Group (facilitator and FRIEND Lunch Group)	Daily support may be needed initially but support is faded over time	**Evaluate the program: Are the kids having fun? What can make the program more enjoyable to all participants?** • Help students feel confident and comfortable with each other • Use opportunities provided in the natural environment to teach, model, prompt, and support interaction between students • Measure the student's present level of functioning, areas of progress, and focus of needed intervention

Who attends the planning meeting will vary according to student needs and school resources. If the student has an IEP, the team should participate in planning the FLP. Key participants in FRIEND® planning meetings may include:

- parent(s) of the student
- paraprofessional/support aide
- lead regular education teacher
- lead special education teacher
- inclusion facilitator or manager
- resource teacher
- speech therapist
- occupational therapist
- school psychologist
- school social worker.

Step 1: identify staff

Early in planning, it's essential for the group to identify a *program supervisor*—someone with the skills, time, and commitment to drive the program forward. Speech therapists, school psychologists, or resource teachers make excellent supervisors because they have strong clinical skills. As the supervisor is primarily responsible for planning the program, a *program facilitator* will also need to be identified. The facilitator is usually a dedicated aide or talented graduate student and is the person who works with the students directly. For the sake of consistency, the program supervisor and facilitator may be the same individuals identified in the FPP.

An effective program supervisor will ensure that the program is implemented with fidelity and ensures data collection to measure progress. Flexibility, positive energy, enthusiasm, and a sense of humor go a long way to ensure the program's success as well.

The program facilitator is guided by the supervisor and implements the program daily. The facilitator will ensure that students are seated together and will provide the support necessary to encourage appropriate social communication. In consultation with the supervisor, the facilitator will strategically fade support as the student begins independently engaging with peers appropriately, but still remain in close proximity to ensure ongoing success. Support may need to be increased or decreased at various times throughout the school year. These decisions should be made during the FLP meetings, but the facilitator monitors the progress and reports back to the group. The talent and skill of facilitators will vary, which is why guidance, supervision, and structure by a skilled professional are essential. See Appendix VI for Implementation Checklists.

Step 2: select peers

Researchers and educators have long recognized that peers are an underutilized, but widely available, source of natural support in every school. Peer-mediated approaches have been an effective intervention strategy in classrooms for as long as there have been schools (Harper and Maheady, 2007).

However, it takes more than increased proximity to ensure that students actually interact with and get to know each other. Students' attitudes about their classmates with ASD do not necessarily change simply because they are enrolled in the same classes (Siperstein, Norins, and Mohler, 2007). Thoughtful, well-planned interventions are necessary in this effort. The FLP creates a context within which interactions between students with social challenges and their classmates are encouraged, facilitated, and supported.

Finding the right number of peers is an essential component to the program and is largely dependent on the individual needing support. We recommend no more than four to six students should be involved in the group at one time. Ideally, the FRIEND® Lunch Group should appear similar to typical groups of students. A student who is more severely impaired may benefit from a slightly larger group of peer participants. That is, if the student is very impaired, the peers (while they want to help) may be more reluctant to spend lunchtime with him or her every day. A few extra peers in the group may allow for flexibility in ongoing support. Less socially challenged students will benefit from the strategic support provided by a group of three to four peers. Involving too many peers might be counterproductive, as the peers may interact more with each other than with the student with social challenges. Thus the number of FLP peer participants may vary depending on the needs of the student with social challenges.

Although there is no single right way to identify typical peers for the FLP, certain strategies can help ensure success (see Table 6.2 below). Social networks change over time, even for typical children, and the reasons may not always be apparent to adults. It is important that this process is flexible and responsive to changes that may occur naturally during the school year. The ultimate goal is to make the program interesting and fun, with enough structure and support for all participants to feel comfortable, so that everyone wants to be involved.

Table 6.2 has been modified from *Peer Support Strategies* (Carter, Cushing, and Kennedy, 2009).

Table 6.2 Selecting FRIEND® peer participants

Preference of students with social challenges

• Who does the student want to spend time with? If a student has limited communication skills, a teacher might:
  – observe which classmates a student gravitates toward, or
  – provide small group opportunities to determine who like working together
• The student may know peers from his or her community. He or she may feel more comfortable inviting familiar people into the FRIEND Program

Age of peer participants
• Just like typical students, a student with social challenges is most likely to have things in common with other students of approximately the same age • If possible, peer participants should be enrolled in the same classroom so they have other things in common
Interest
• The most successful peer support arrangements are those in which all students are enthusiastic about working together • Not every student will want to be a peer participant, and no one should be compelled to assume this role • Peers may be hesitant to get involved with FRIEND because they don't know how to support a student with social challenges • Have students indicate on a postcard if they are interested in participating in the program. The postcard can be distributed again at a later date; students who observe the group having fun may change their minds about participating
Shared interests
• The more students have in common, the more likely they are to develop relationships that extend outside the classroom • Some common interests might include a mutual interest in sports, a favorite band or style of music, a common hobby, a shared group of friends, similar religious beliefs, or living in the same neighborhood

cont.

Peers with friends
• Peer participants who are part of an already existing group of friends are more likely to introduce the student to other students
• If possible, and the peer group is willing, the student can join an existing group of friends

Interpersonal skills
• Peer participants who have the following qualities are excellent models: friendliness, the ability to get along with others, confidence, respect, empathy, patience, and sensitivity
• Peers who struggle with some of these same characteristics may gain these skills from the FLP, along with the student with social challenges

Gender of peer participants
• At this age, children are more likely to make friends with same sex peers
• Although young girls often like to "mother" kids with special needs, a male student with challenges will need to learn how to act, talk, and feel comfortable with other boys at school

One day on the playground, Brian was attempting to shoot hoops alone. One of his classmates approached him and began showing him how to hold and follow through with the ball. He treated Brian just like his other classmates and seemed to enjoy the interaction.

At the end of recess, I thanked the boy for helping Brian and complemented his basketball skills. He seemed surprised but appreciated the positive feedback. Later I discovered that he is a student with his own behavioral challenges in the classroom.

After I acknowledged his support of Brian, he played basketball with him more often. He would pass the ball to him and give him opportunities to practice the skills he learned. His friends also started playing with them. Brian's confidence and skills improved with the assistance and support of his peers. They formed the perfect FRIEND® Lunch Group without any adult guidance or supervision. I realized, "Kids really want to do this kind of thing."

Appropriate peers can be identified in several different ways. On the playground, the student with social challenges may be observed gravitating toward a few peers, but may not be successful with the interaction. These students may be suitable participants as peers in the FLP. Peers can also be identified through the Social Functioning Interview (see Chapter 4 and Appendix III), which includes a section for respondents to indicate a preference toward particular classmates.

For an older child or adolescent who has a particular interest (e.g. chess, theater, computers), a school club for those special interests can create a natural community of support. The process of selecting FRIEND® Lunch Group peer participants is important and requires some attention, but shouldn't slow down the program implementation. Once the peers are identified they will need to build their social skills to be effective members of the program.

Once a group of candidates for the FLP has been identified, a letter is sent home to the peers' parents. This letter describes the FLP, and requests permission for participation from the peers' parents. Contact information for the school's FLP supervisor should be included in the letter, so any questions and concerns can be addressed. See the draft letter in Appendix I.

Step 3: training and supervision
Getting started
An orientation and initial training will help peer participants become prepared and committed to the FRIEND Lunch Group. Regular meetings with educational staff provide peers with a safe and confidential place to ask questions and receive feedback and ideas for possible strategies based on the facilitator's observations during the lunch period.

The student with social challenges will also need an initial orientation and training session. As the FLP gets underway the student may need to communicate concerns. It's important that the student with social challenges feel comfortable and supported in the FLP.

Both of these meetings are important to the success of the program because they open communication between staff and students. It is best if they are held separately and privately to encourage open communication without judgment from each other.

It is important for the peers to recognize that they need to encourage the student to act independently whenever possible. Doing so will provide many opportunities to practice skills in a supportive environment. The peers should never feel like they are in the group to do things for the student with social challenges. They need to teach by example and support as necessary.

Peer participants will assume various roles depending on the specific needs of the student with social challenges. Orientation and training should include an individualized component. However, it may be useful to address some common issues with all participating students. These issues can be addressed in an orientation meeting, which may be broken into two sessions. A general outline of this orientation session is provided in Table 6.3.

Table 6.3 Outline of the orientation session

Introduction to the program

• Collect parent permission slips
• Provide a brief explanation of the program:
  – Students will eat lunch together every day
  – Students will support and help each other throughout the day
  – The group will get together at a pre-arranged location for the FRIEND® group meeting to play games, eat snacks or lunch, and talk about how things are going on a regular basis (weekly, every two weeks or monthly)
• Discuss what each student has to offer to the program and why they are interested

Rules

• Create rules for participation
• Create a chart or write rules that can be referred to in the future
• Sample rules:
  – Everything discussed must remain confidential
  – All students will be treated with respect
  – Speak kindly and honestly about each other
  – The group will eat lunch together and support the student with social challenges at various times throughout the school day (e.g. between classes or on the school bus)

Introduce the target student

• Discuss inclusion of target student in the group:
  – Invite students to talk about positive characteristics of student (e.g. knows a lot about a subject, is friendly) and help students find common interests within the group
  – Invite students to think about challenges they may have (e.g. spelling, math, baseball)
  – Discuss some possible challenges the target student may have (e.g. sitting alone at recess, acting a little odd sometimes, not responding to statements)
  – Remind peer participants that everyone needs help sometimes and everyone has some gift, talent, or skill they can share with others
  – During discussion explain why some of the challenges exist *(with permission of parent and as agreed by the IEP team)*—discuss autism. May include content from peer sensitivity training

Strategies

• Discuss ways peers can be supportive:
  – Review "Tips for Peers" (Appendix V)
  – Provide suggestions for motivating the student with social differences
  – Role play to practice problem solving; provide feedback to peers
  – Introduce instructional strategies such as modeling, prompting, and corrective feedback

Summary and conclusion
• Allow time for the peer participants to ask questions • Be sure peers understand there will be time to practice new skills; they don't need to remember everything from orientation • Remind the students of who they can go to for assistance and questions • Review the schedule for the peer participants to meet

Teaching peers to provide social support

It is essential that all FRIEND® peer participants become knowledgeable and confident in their abilities to support a student with social challenges. While some FRIEND peer participants will have intuitive skills in supporting their classmates, all will benefit from support and information as needed.

Do not underestimate the skills peers can naturally bring to this process. Remember, they are already social experts! The research literature clearly demonstrates the capacity of students to support their peers (Bass and Mulick, 2007; Goldstein *et al.*, 2007; Harper *et al.*, 2008; McGee *et al.*, 1992; Nelson *et al.*, 2007; Owen-DeSchryver *et al.*, 2008). The current generation of students has grown up attending inclusive schools and classrooms, and is experienced at working collaboratively. Recently, students have demonstrated improved attitudes toward, and increased willingness to get to know, their classmates with disabilities (Fisher, 1999; Krajewski, Hyde, and O'Keefe, 2002).

Be flexible

Peer participants don't need to know everything about the program on the first day. The process of education and support is best when it is provided over time, and information may be given in response to a particular question or event. The students will learn best through observation, guidance, and support from the supervisor and facilitator.

Training and support for peer participants should be tailored to the challenges of the student they are supporting. The focus of the program should emerge from the baseline assessments and goals on the student's IEP. It is not the peer participants' job to be clinical interventionists, but rather to provide opportunities for the student to practice social-communication skills throughout the school day. The peer participants might introduce the student to other peers in the classroom, teach him or her a joke, give practical advice, provide emotional support, or make after-school plans. Peer participants should be encouraged to engage in activities the student is interested in. The peers can learn things and benefit from this relationship too.

CREATE PURPOSE
The manner in which the FRIEND® Lunch Group is introduced to the peer participants will determine how they think about the relationship between themselves and the student with social challenges. Supervisors or facilitators should explain to peers that they are to provide examples of socialization to the student and offer support. Their role in the program is to be friends, not teachers or caregivers.

Peer participants should learn to provide the least amount of support necessary to encourage a student with challenges to participate independently in an activity or interaction (Carter et al., 2009). At the peer participant support meetings, school staff can introduce strategies for the peers to provide support.

Step 4: implementation
Intervention strategies
Peers should be given the tools and resources to be a social mentor. The more they know, the more effective the program will be.

PROMPTING
Peer participants can help a classmate learn by using natural prompts when teaching a new skill. There are several types of prompts a peer participant might use including modeling, verbal, gesture, and proximity (Maurice, Green, and Luce, 1996):

- Modeling is when a peer shows the target student how to play a game or do a particular activity by demonstrating it. While some students will be able to learn something by watching an activity, other students may not know how to imitate. These students will need more direct prompting strategies and peers can provide this instruction in a natural way.

- A verbal prompt is when a peer tells a target student what they should do. For example, during conversation at lunch, a peer participant can model appropriate conversational skills by telling his or her classmates what he or she thought of the recent Harry Potter movie. He or she may verbally prompt the student by asking him or her what he or she thought of the movie.

- A gesture prompt may be used by a peer to indicate what the target student should do. This could include physical gestures, use of eye gaze, or facial expressions. For example, a peer may look at the target student when it is his or her turn to respond.

- Proximity prompts include strategically placing an item to cue the target student to display a particular behavior. For example, a peer may place a napkin next to the target student during lunch to remind him or her to wipe his or her mouth. Body positioning is another example; a peer may stand closer to the target student when it is time for him or her to move forward in the lunch line.

It is important that peers are taught how to select appropriate prompts. If the target student does not respond to a prompt, a more direct prompt is needed. For example, a verbal prompt is more direct than modeling, and modeling is more direct than gesturing. However, if the level of support is too direct the student with challenges could become dependent on his or her peers. Peers need to learn to fade prompts and allow the student to practice skills. This skill is not easy, but with the appropriate supervision and support from staff, the peers will learn it quickly.

IMPORTANCE OF PRAISE

If a student was completing a mathematics assignment, his or her teacher would give feedback with a grade. When completing a jigsaw puzzle, a young child learns he or she is successful when all the pieces fit together correctly. The challenge in social situations is that success may not be obvious, and there may be a relative lack of positive feedback. When a peer is interacting with a student, a conscious effort should be made to point out and comment on the student's appropriate behavior (Attwood, 2007).

Corrective feedback

In friendships with typically developing peers, one of the most important benefits to the student with social challenges is immediate (and hopefully appropriate) feedback. Peer participants need to be taught how to give helpful and motivating feedback. The strategies in Table 6.4 can be helpful when teaching peer mentors how to provide feedback to students with social challenges.

Table 6.4 Teaching peers how to provide feedback

• Offer positive feedback first, before giving negative feedback: "That was really great that you asked Rory to play the game. Next time try saying Rory's name." Rather than, "Say his name!"
• Focus comments on behaviors rather than on the person: "I like it when you look at me when you talk to me." Instead of, "You look weird when you don't make eye contact."
• Suggest possibilities and alternatives, such as, "I was wondering if…" or "Do you think it might…" rather than saying, "You should have…" or "I would have done it this way…"

• Provide constructive feedback. Praise is most effective when it:
  – is specific: clearly identifying a behavior
  – is frequent: occurring often
  – is contingent: immediately following the desired behavior
  – is varied: praise seems more genuine when it varies with situations

Adapted from Cowie and Wallace (2000)

FRIEND® group meeting

I started attending my brother's FRIEND program when I started high school. I lived my life with him and I was used to his bizarre idiosyncrasies and socially inappropriate behavior, but I worried about what other kids would think of him. I walked in the first day not knowing what to expect. I was the first one there, but within the first few minutes of the lunch period, my brother, Gareth, and four other kids found their way into the classroom we had commandeered for the program. I only knew one of them, besides Gareth. He was a junior, and he had brought along some of his friends who were also juniors. We ate pizza and drank soda, stuff that was way better than the cafeteria fare. Afterward we just talked about whatever; normal stuff, really, movies, sports, video games. Gareth chatted with the other kids as comfortably as I could have hoped and they were doing their best to keep him involved in the conversation. I began to feel more comfortable and settled into my lunch. I was very happy to find out that these kids understood Gareth's differences, and accepted them.

While the group should eat lunch together every day in the lunchroom, with all the other students, it is necessary to have regular "check-in" meetings (bi-monthly or monthly) to address problems and keep the program interesting. The FRIEND® Lunch Group check-in meeting includes peer participants, the student with social challenges, and the FLP facilitator (or designee). These meetings help build cohesiveness and problem solving in a fun environment. To increase their commitment and interest in the activities, invite students to suggest their favorite games. This is a great time to celebrate successes with a snack or special treat and make improvements to other strategies. We realize that parents (and schools) may have limited resources, but a special lunch (pizza) or a snack during the meeting is a great social motivator. Table 6.5 gives strategies for improving cohesiveness of a FRIEND group.

Table 6.5 Strategies for improving FRIEND® group cohesiveness

- Help the students develop a sense of purpose for the FRIEND Lunch Group
- Adult support of the program will help students feel pride in membership
- Help FRIEND Lunch Group members think of ways to work together
- Help the group understand and appreciate each other's strengths
- Build a sense of camaraderie though fun shared activities
- Talk openly about what is working well in the FLP, as well as how the program can be improved

Daily lunch group

While getting a group of students together to eat lunch sounds simple, it will be more effective to think of the FRIEND Lunch Group as a form of therapy for the student with social challenges. This kind of approach will help you remember to pay attention to the small details of each meeting. Listed below are some of the details that need attention to maintain a successful program; these may seem obvious, but are easily overlooked. A supervisor should routinely observe the Lunch Group to ensure the facilitator is implementing the program with fidelity (Appendix VI).

SEATING ARRANGEMENT

Seating arrangement is an important component of the FRIEND® group meeting. The facilitator should make sure the group members are sitting together. While we want all the participants to be seated where they are most comfortable, we also want to ensure the student with social challenges is at the center of the group rather than sitting near the group. This location will make it easier to interact with peers.

TOPIC SELECTION

The FRIEND Lunch Group should look just like a group of students sitting and talking together at a lunch table, but it may be a little difficult to get started. The facilitator should help make it fun and easy by adding structure. For example, at the FRIEND Lunch Group check-in meeting the students can make conversation sticks: everyone writes down a conversation topic on a Popsicle stick. Then every day at lunch two to three sticks are picked and students start a conversation. Similar to this activity, a spinner can be adapted, or a chart created for dice to select various conversation topics. Making these games can be fun and really get students engaged in the program. Playing the games at lunch creates the opportunity to practice conversation skills. These activities also create the opportunity to shift to other topics and not remain focused for too long, which is a common problem among individuals with social challenges.

ENSURE PARTICIPATION OF ALL STUDENTS

Once a conversation has started, it is important to create opportunities for everyone to participate. The facilitator should ensure each child is asked a question before the topic is changed, or have students ask the person to their right about the last movie they saw. If there is an item that will be passed out during the FRIEND Lunch Group, have one participant hold all the items and each of the other students make an appropriate request. For example, if pizza is brought in for the group meeting, have the target student ask each peer what type of slice they want and pass out the pizza accordingly. For some FRIEND groups, this level of facilitation is not needed. Observe the conversation and ensure that all students are participating.

FADE SUPPORT WHEN POSSIBLE

The goal of the FRIEND Lunch Group is to teach the target student to engage appropriately with peers during lunch. Support and encouragement are critical during this process. It is also essential that the facilitator and peers fade support during the school year to encourage skill development.

PROVIDE SPECIFIC PRAISE

A facilitator should not miss an opportunity to praise any group member. Any time someone spontaneously offers to share with a peer, or asks the target student a question, the facilitator should provide direct praise, letting the student know what he or she did and what was good about it. Praise or preferred items should be provided within a few seconds of the behavior. The facilitator should also label the appropriate behavior so the students clearly understand what they did well. Once a skill is taught, the facilitator needs to provide opportunities for the students to practice this behavior repeatedly, and praise should be given each time.

Table 6.6 lists additional strategies to support students with social challenges and their peers in the FRIEND® Lunch Group.

Table 6.6 Effective social skill strategies

- Fade prompts as quickly as possible to allow time for practice
- Vary the instruction method and strategies when teaching skills according to the individual needs of the students
- Teach self-monitoring strategies which help students recognize and track their own behaviors
- Practice learned skills in multiple settings continuously
- Explain why the learned skill is important and useful

Parent involvement

Through the information shared at the ongoing staff–parent meetings, the team can discuss opportunities for the student with social differences to be "primed" at home on materials that will support his or her emerging social communication skills.

During lunch the facilitator observed peers talking about a popular TV show. The student with social challenges, Cory, had never watched the show, and was missing an opportunity to engage with peers and build conversational skills. When Cory's parents learned about the peer participants' interest, they introduced the show to their son. In fact, his entire family watched the show together and talked about it at various times throughout the day so that Cory would better understand the plot and characters. This increased his enjoyment of the show and gave him a lot of material for conversations during lunch.

The target student's parents can also inform the school staff about their child's special interests and abilities. Activities in the FLP built around these interests will increase the student's motivation to participate.

Step 5: supervision
FRIEND® Lunch Group check-in meetings
Supervision for the FRIEND Lunch Group is ongoing and embedded in training, implementation, and FRIEND Lunch Group check-in meetings. Initially, the FRIEND program supervisor will want to use the "FRIEND Lunch Checklist" in Appendix VI to ensure that the program facilitator is implementing the program with fidelity. The Observation Recording Form in Appendix IV can be used frequently to collect data on a student's response to their treatment plan. Training and implementation should be modified based on a student's progress (or lack of) so that interventions are meaningful and precise. Data and strategies are shared with parents so that social skills can be primed and interventions can be extended to home and community.

The FRIEND Lunch Group check-in meeting provides an ongoing opportunity for supervision and problem solving with the program supervisor, facilitator, peers, and student with social challenges. A great way to keep students motivated is to ensure the group meetings are fun and interactive. Activities should be geared to the shared interests of all participants and provide an opportunity to celebrate the participation of the group. The key is to keep things simple and when possible, novel. There are numerous ways to come up with ideas for activities. Books or the internet are great resources for ideas of age-appropriate activities. Just be sure all activities are age appropriate for all group members.

CHAPTER SUMMARY

✓ Spend time observing typical students at lunch to determine how to set up an FLP that is similar to naturally occurring groups. The number of peer participants should be comparable to a naturally occurring group of friends.

✓ Methods for selecting peers include using suggestions from the student with social challenges, parents, and educators from the Social Functioning Interviews. A school club based on special interests might create a natural community of support for an older student with social challenges.

✓ Consider the following characteristics when selecting peer participants: preference of the student with social challenges, age of the peer participants (should be similar to the age of the target student), interest, willingness to learn, same gender, varying abilities, and prior experience or exposure to individuals with social challenges

✓ Effective teaching and support of peer participants will be provided in response to a particular student's needs while they are interacting with the student at lunchtime during FRIEND® Lunch Group check-in meetings.

✓ Peers should be encouraged to provide support not supervision, be a friend not a teacher, and offer help not care.

✓ At orientation, Daily Lunch Groups, and FRIEND Lunch Group check-in meetings the supervisor and facilitator will review and practice basic intervention strategies with peers: modeling, prompting, and offering choices, appropriate praise and corrective feedback.

✓ Facilitators need to ensure the Daily Lunch Group is seated together, facilitate conversation around interest of peers, create opportunities for communication, provide support to the target student as needed, reinforce all appropriate social behaviors, and practice appropriate social skills as opportunities occur.

✓ FLP meetings are important to maintain all students' desire to participate in the program. Select activities that are highly preferred by the target student, yet mutually enjoyable for all the group members. When necessary, activities should be modified to support everyone's participation.

7

The FRIEND®
Playground Program

My daughters, Caitlyn and Hailey, are identical twins and they have autism. In their early years, I worried a lot about their ability to learn to talk, read, write, and do all the things that would be necessary for them to go to school. Although traditional school subjects continue to be a challenge, at some point my concerns shifted to their socialization. The girls pretty much stuck to themselves at school; they rarely talked to other children and other children seldom spoke to them.

I knew that socializing would only get harder in the years to come. How would they ever learn to get along with peers? How would they ever get a job? I knew from employment reports that adults with autism were most likely to be fired because of their poor social skills. I knew we had to do something to help them now.

I expressed my concerns to the principal and with support from me and other parents we started FRIEND®. Autism professionals trained school personnel to be "social coaches" on the playground and to collect data to measure progress. In the span of a few weeks, the girls went from being alone on the playground to engaging in a variety of activities with many new friends. At drop-off, instead of hugging the fence or staying by themselves, one girl raced off to play soccer and the other was quickly embraced by a circle of friends. All along, they wanted to socialize, they just didn't know how.

INTRODUCTION

A playground can be a place for fun, games, and friendship development. It can also be a place for loneliness, bullying, and other problem behavior. Playground time is typically an unstructured environment for students, with only a few staff members to supervise playground activity. However, even with a few staff members to help add structure, the playground can become an optimal setting for students with social challenges to develop their social skills.

According to the American Academy of Pediatrics (2013), recess offers a unique form of cognitive, social, emotional, and physical benefits that are often underappreciated. Recess is a crucial and necessary component of a child's development and, as such, it should never be withheld for punitive or academic reasons. All too often students may hear, "Finish your work or no recess," or "You misbehaved so you need to stay in at recess." This kind of punitive action is probably even more common among students with cognitive, behavioral, or social challenges. Even if they are on the playground, the unstructured environment may be too difficult to navigate.

Students with social challenges may not have the skills necessary to get the full benefit of playground activities. In addition to social challenges these students may also have poor motor skills. Weaker motor skills in students with ASD were found to correlate with higher severity of the disorder (MacDonald, Lord, and Ulrich 2013). It's easy to see how these students get left out or even avoid others. As a result, these students have fewer opportunities to develop the social and play skills needed to be successful.

At the same time, students participating in sports like soccer or games like four-square were found to be more successful in social communication than students who did not have these play skills (Kasari *et al.*, 2010). The relationship between motor skills and social communicative challenges needs to be further explored. Still, it's crucial that social skill building programs like FRIEND® include activities students need to improve their motor and play skills.

By providing structured activities with a social coach (facilitator), the unstructured playground now provides opportunities for all students to join in group activities that promote social interaction and engagement. An additional benefit to structured playground activities is the reduction of problem behaviors. If there is more supervision and more structure, there will be less opportunity for bullying, teasing or fighting. School personnel will spend more time on productive activities for students instead of discipline.

In this chapter we will present guidelines for training playground supervisors (school personnel, parent volunteers, or paraprofessionals) to add structure to the playground and suggest ideas for activities to support students with social challenges. Perhaps the most important aspect of any program is the data collection so we will provide suggestions on how to collect data easily.

THE FPP IMPLEMENTATION
Planning

The FRIEND® Planning Meeting allows educators, professionals, parents, and aides to plan and coordinate assessments and interventions for Peer Sensitivity, the Lunch Program, and the Playground Program. As FRIEND evolves, be sure to integrate all aspects of the program with all team members.

Step 1: identify staff
PROGRAM SUPERVISOR

An FPP supervisor will ensure that the program is implemented correctly. The supervisor identifies effective facilitators, trains them, and provides ongoing feedback. Potential program supervisors are the school psychologist, speech and language pathologist, school counselor, a teacher or therapist, or someone who has experience in leadership and training. The supervisor should oversee data collection and analysis, delegating various tasks, and making data-driven decisions to ensure the efficacy of the program.

FACILITATOR

The playground facilitator is the person who brings structured activities to the playground. There may be one facilitator or many playground facilitators depending on the number of students with social challenges. Facilitators are not there just to play with the students, but are to create activities that encourage students to play with students. It could be someone who is already providing services to the student, like an aide or paraprofessional.

Support provided to the target students may need to be increased at various times throughout the school year; the playground facilitator should monitor this need and adjust the level of support accordingly. When the target student needs less support, the playground facilitator should still continue to set up structured activities, supervise, collect data, and support the student.

If resources permit, all recess periods should have a facilitator who adds structure for those students who would otherwise have challenges playing with peers. The more the program is implemented, the more learning opportunities will be created for the students with social challenges, and the more progress will be seen.

We recognize that school resources and personnel may be limited, so you may need to get creative when identifying personnel for this program. Other suggestions for facilitators might be rotating teachers who volunteer their time on different days of the week. For some students with ASD, a behavior interventionist may be contracted from a local agency. The local community college or university may provide an internship through their academic program that allows undergraduate or graduate students to be playground facilitators.

While it seems obvious, it is still worth mentioning that the playground facilitator needs to have play skills and enjoy playing with children. A facilitator who enjoys interacting with students will entice more students to join playground activities. Attracting typical peers to playground activities is key to a successful program. A variety of activities and peers provides many learning opportunities for students with challenges. Furthermore, it is essential to designate individuals who do not have other responsibilities during recess time. That is, a safety monitor would not be able to provide direct implementation of this program as a facilitator. Table 7.1 shows the roles and possible personnel for these roles.

Table 7.1 The FRIEND® Playground supervisor and facilitator roles

Staff	Training	Role
FRIEND® playground supervisor	School psychologist Speech and language pathologist Counselor Resource teacher or therapist	• Oversee data collection and analysis • Delegate tasks to playground facilitator • Collect data on playground facilitator to ensure program fidelity • Make data-driven decisions • Coordinate interventions with FRIEND Lunch staff

Playground facilitator	School aide	• Act as a playground facilitator
	Para-professional	• Facilitate structured activities and adapt as needed to encourage independence
	Graduate student-intern	
	Volunteer teacher	• Collect data as directed by playground supervisor
	Behavior interventionist	

Step 2: training and supervision

Before starting intervention, the playground facilitator(s) should receive basic training on social challenges, applied behavior analysis (ABA)-based interventions, and the need for data collection. As we have said before, data-driven decisions about all aspects of FRIEND® are critical to successful implementation.

Facilitators need to be careful about providing too much structure for too long. Instead, they need to learn the importance of fading supports and encouraging more independence, which is a critical element of the FPP. FRIEND is not just about support, but also about learning and developing skills for independence. Once a student enjoys structured activities, the facilitator needs to adapt the structure gradually to encourage the student's independence. Easier said than done! This kind of approach requires training and practice.

After training, facilitators should spend time on the playground meeting with both the students with social challenges and typical peers. They can begin to observe functioning with an analytical eye and get ideas about where to begin. The facilitator should pay attention to which playground activities students enjoy. What are the student's interests? The facilitator can also talk with the student's peers about activities they might want to do in the future.

Step 3: implementation

During lunch/recess Rafael ate by himself and then sat alone by the lunch boxes rather than play with other students. As a playground monitor, I asked Rafael if he wanted to go play during one recess period. He told me he did not like to play and would just wait for recess to be over. I talked to Rafael about what he liked to play at home and he told me he was very interested in board games.

The next day I brought some games to lunch and we played one together. I realized that Rafael looked different by playing a board game with an adult, so I invited some other students to play with him. Each day new peers would join the group and play games with Rafael. Soon, I only needed to stand by and observe. During the rest of the school year he and the group played other playground games like four-square, Red Light/Green Light. It never took Rafael 45 minutes to finish his lunch again.

PROVIDE STRUCTURE

The playground facilitator's first objective will be to add structure to the unstructured playground. This task can be approached by introducing a new activity or finding an existing activity that students are playing on their own, then adding structure to make it more inclusive.

FOLLOW THE STUDENT'S LEAD

A student in the FPP liked to tie hula hoops to the playground fence with jump ropes. After unsuccessfully attempting to engage him in activities with his peers, the playground facilitator determined she should incorporate his interest into an activity that would also interest his peers. The hula hoops became targets. Peers would throw a ball at the fence and try to get the ball in the hula hoops. Initially the student with social challenges only wanted to help make the targets, but eventually he started taking turns with peers throwing the balls.

Another student who was particularly difficult to engage liked to sweep with a broom. So, using toy brooms, the playground facilitator set up relay races with the brooms and tennis balls. Not only did the student love this activity but many of his peers enjoyed racing with him.

It is important to remember that playground activities are not mandatory for any student to attend. Therefore, when selecting games and activities, the playground facilitator should follow the lead of the students. Many students with ASD prefer activities with a strong sensory component so they may enjoy playground activities that involve running, jumping, or swinging (Doody and Mertz, 2013). Structuring an activity based on student suggestions or offering games that are geared toward the interest of a student will increase his or her motivation. It is important to have several activities planned. A facilitator needs to be flexible and creative. If students are not interested in the planned activities, the playground facilitator should try something else. A good strategy is to simply ask students what they would like to do.

Students with social challenges are often drawn to adults and will easily engage in activities with the playground facilitator. A facilitator should take care to avoid being the student's playmate, but shouldn't just supervise either. In the beginning of the program, a facilitator may participate as long as more than one student is engaged in the activity. Keep in mind the goal of the program is to increase students' engagement with each other, not with adults.

MATERIALS AND EQUIPMENT

While it is not necessary to have equipment to implement this program, it is certainly helpful. Activities that involve Frisbees, balls, rackets, and so on attract a variety of students, making structured activities more fun and attractive. Materials also provide a natural way to facilitate social communication between students. If one student has all of the sand shovels, other students will need to ask that student to gain access to them. Materials can also be helpful when teaching turn taking. If there is only one basketball, students must learn to take turns so that all students who are interested in playing basketball can participate.

If materials and equipment are not available, activities such as: Duck, Duck, Goose; Red Light/Green Light; tag; Red Rover, and relay races can be facilitated on the playground. These activities also require turn taking and provide many opportunities to practice appropriate social behavior.

IDEAS FOR ACTIVITIES

The best method for developing activity ideas is simply to ask the students what they like doing at recess. You can do this informally on the playground with just a few students or collect data from a larger group of students with a survey. While it is important to expand the number of activities in students' repertoire, this approach is a good starting place. Facilitators can develop ideas from successful interactions that occur during activities. However, teaching new games does not make a facilitator successful. Incorporating the student's interest into games (to make the game more motivating) is more important.

Table 7.2 provides a sample list of activities for students in elementary school, middle school, or high school. These are some ideas to get the facilitator's creative juices flowing. For other ideas there are plenty of resources, websites, and books that identify fun playground activities. The point is to encourage facilitators to choose games that have a social component (i.e. turn taking and working together) and are somewhat age appropriate. It would obviously look silly for a group of sixth grade students to play Duck, Duck, Goose as well as being less motivating to typical peers.

Table 7.2 Suggested playground activities

Playground activities	Board games	Sports
Four-square	Jenga	Soccer
Hopscotch	Lucky Ducks	Catch
Jump rope	Bingo	Football
Duck, Duck, Goose	Don't Break the Ice	Baseball/Tee ball
Red Rover	Operation	Kickball
Red Light/Green Light	Connect Four	Basketball
Simon Says	Memory	Dodgeball
Capture the Flag	Uno	Volleyball
Freeze tag	Ants in the Pants	Bowling
Buddy tag	Tic-Tac-Toe	Croquet
TV tag	Twister	Frisbee golf
Scavenger hunt		Soccer
Charades		Ultimate Frisbee
Freeze dance		Wall-ball
Bean bag toss		
Chalk		
Construction toys		

CREATE OPPORTUNITIES FOR ENGAGEMENT

After introducing the activity, the facilitator should find opportunities for students to play cooperatively. For example, students drawing with chalk on the playground are probably each doing their own thing. While they might be having fun, they are engaging in parallel play; participating in the same activity near their peers, but not *with* their peers. To make this activity more cooperative and encourage social communication between students, the playground facilitator can designate one child to be in charge of the chalk. If anyone wants to play with the chalk, he will need to ask the student who holds the chalk for a piece. This provides students with an opportunity to initiate with a peer. It also provides an opportunity for the student with the chalk to practice responding to peers.

Students may also work together to create one large picture with the chalk. For example, if the target student likes sea life, the students can work together to create an underwater scene. One student can draw a fish, while another draws the water, and still another draws plants. By having students work together, a parallel play activity is transformed into a cooperative play activity. This provides an increased number of opportunities for social communication and social skills practice.

Another way to increase opportunities for students to engage with each other is to start a game where one student does something and the other students need to guess, like charades. If students engage together in an activity, they can practice initiating and responding to one another, turn taking, and good sportsmanship.

PROVIDE SUPPORT

It is important that playground facilitators are constantly monitoring social interactions of all students in the program to see where support is needed. The facilitators need to provide an appropriate level of support according to the needs of the target students. Some students may not be able to initiate even a simple interaction and may need structured prompts to learn. Other students may be able to initiate, but may need encouragement to find a playmate. In both cases the facilitator should encourage the initiation then add support to the interaction. The facilitator can provide verbal prompting to initiate with peers. If the student has the skills but doesn't use them, he or she may not feel confident in the outcome. The structure of FRIEND® will help improve that student's confidence to initiate and play with peers successfully. Table 7.3 summarizes the Playground Facilitator's playground responsibilities.

Table 7.3 The playground facilitator's responsibilities

Facilitator's responsibilities	Interventions
Continual playground assessment	• Observe and speak to students with social challenges and typical peers to get ideas about where to begin • Which playground activities do students enjoy? • What are the students' interests? • What activities might students want to do in the future?

cont.

Facilitator's responsibilities	Interventions
Create structure on the playground	• Have a few activities planned; however, if students aren't interested, expand or adapt current activities • Many students with ASD prefer activities with a strong sensory component so they may enjoy playground activities that involve running, jumping, or swinging • Modify parallel play activities into cooperative activities: chalk art project, charades, relay races
Provide support (directly or by encouraging peers)	• Prompt, model, offer choice, and provide appropriate praise and corrective feedback to students with social challenges and typical peers • Encourage typical peers to engage student(s) with social challenges by using the same strategies • Provide daily opportunities to teach, support, and practice social and play skills • Practice appropriate behavior after problem behavior has occurred
Encourage independence	• Be helpful, but not too helpful • Goal is for student with social challenges to play with peers, not playground facilitator • Teach skills student needs to initiate and maintain play • Encourage independence by prompting, "Find someone to play with." Student will decide what to play and who to play with

JUGGLING MULTIPLE STUDENTS

If there is more than one student who needs support on the playground, the facilitator needs to make judgments about skill levels of each student. If two students need a lot of support, it may be better to spend a long period of time with one student during a specific recess time, and work with the other student during another recess time. This approach might be more effective than quickly moving back and forth between the two students every recess period. Depending on the demand, help from other staff or maybe mature peers might be necessary.

REINFORCE APPROPRIATE BEHAVIOR

A playground facilitator will need to provide reinforcement for appropriate social behavior on the playground. The facilitator can praise a student who is cheering on his or her peers during a kickball game. The facilitator can give the student a gold star (or the equivalent) or send a note home to his or her parents to let them know how he or she helped a student with social challenges at recess. If a student shows good sportsmanship on the playground, let him or her know that because of his or her good behavior, he or she can be team captain the next day.

PROBLEM BEHAVIORS

It was almost a daily occurrence for Mike, a third grade student with ASD, to get in trouble for bothering his peers during recess. He would often get close to peers and scream at them. Since most of Mike's interactions were annoying to his peers, they would stay away from him. It was well known that Mike's favorite activity on the playground was to run and be chased; however, peers would never play with him because he was annoying.

When the FPP was implemented three peers were asked if they would play a game of chase with Mike. They happily agreed and asked him to play. Mike responded with a big smile and said, "Let's play a running game."

When Mike wanted to run with another peer, he screamed in his face, "Run with me!" and the peer was instantly turned off. The playground facilitator then provided feedback and modeled to Mike on how to ask in a nice voice rather than scream a command. Mike then asked the same peer to run with him nicely and he agreed. The facilitator asked the kids if they wanted to play again the next day and they all did. The next day, the playground facilitator set up the game again, and prompted Mike to ask peers to run with him appropriately, without screaming in anyone's face. Mike was successful and everyone had fun.

Problem behaviors, like screaming at other students or grabbing things from them, can prevent social interactions immediately. The facilitator will need to identify these behaviors and set up opportunities for students to practice the appropriate behavior. For example, a student who is playing with markers may grab another marker directly out of a peer's hands. Often, adults try to correct the behavior by repeatedly telling the student, "you need to ask for things," but never provide opportunities for practice of the appropriate behavior. Therefore, it is important to set up the opportunity for the student to practice the appropriate behavior.

The amount of practice required for a student to learn a new behavior will vary from student to student. Some will be more frustrating than others. Tenacity is an important trait for a facilitator. If opportunities are provided frequently, the student will learn a new, appropriate behavior.

USING STUDENT MENTORS

It's always more natural when students learn from peers rather than adults. Thus, the facilitator may recruit students in middle or high school to help and be mentors on the playground. The best student mentors will be motivated to learn about social development and challenges. With only minimal training, student mentors can be ready to go. They need to know how to facilitate games and teach appropriate social interactions. Good play skills with activities that are appropriate for younger students will help too. If the schools are on the same campus, students in middle school can volunteer to help in the program during their lunch period. If the schools agree, perhaps a training program can be arranged where students get credit or recognition for participating. The facilitator will need to monitor mentors to ensure their effectiveness and collect data on their students.

Step 4: supervision

After an initial training period, it's important that facilitators receive continuous training and feedback from the program supervisor. The supervisor should collect data on the facilitator's playground skills so they can provide helpful feedback about what he or she is doing well and highlight areas that need improvement. A form to measure fidelity of implementation is included in Appendix VI. As with any new task, skills for implementation should be taught in a stepwise manner. That is, perhaps only the first two strategies for implementation on the form should be mastered by the facilitator before the additional strategies are incorporated. Regardless of the approach for training, the form will help supervisors document the strengths and challenges of facilitators during implementation.

CHAPTER SUMMARY

✓ The FPP is a structured ABA-based intervention for building motor, play, and social skills. Frequent opportunities for learning will increase the rate of skill acquisition.

✓ There is a relationship between motor skills and social skills. Activities like sports and other playground games provide opportunities to learn and practice social skills. Students with motor skill impairments are at a disadvantage and require support.

✓ The following steps ensure successful implementation: select a playground supervisor to oversee the program, select playground facilitator(s) for daily implementation, provide training to staff on program implementation, and provide supervision on playground skills using the fidelity of implementation form.

✓ Implement program strategies daily: provide structure, follow the student's lead, create opportunities, provide support, and reinforce appropriate behavior.

✓ Suggested playground activities: find age-appropriate activities that match student interests.

✓ While the structure of FRIEND® personnel and activities is important, so is flexibility. Good, effective programs can be developed with the available resources at most schools as long as the principles defined here are applied.

Strategies for Parents

When my parents first told me that my older brother had autism, I didn't really understand what that meant. I was only seven, my brother nine, and to me he seemed pretty normal. I started to notice differences like his very specific diet (overcooked turkey bacon and crunchy cereals) or the occasional odd comment. When we played with friends in the neighborhood Peter's differences really stood out. We would be playing hide and seek and Peter would be off doing his own thing. Remembering my parents' request, I would ask him to join us. Now, Peter is surprisingly social and I believe he got many of his skills from interacting with our neighborhood friends. At 18 he understands social rules and follows them most of the time. I still have to prompt him occasionally, usually not to stare at pretty girls, but less now than before. Encouraging Peter to join in when we were kids helped him learn these skills and significantly improved his current quality of life.

HOMEWORK

Previous chapters focused on opportunities for social communication on the playground and in the lunchroom at school. Of course, these opportunities can occur in situations outside of school too. Clubs and play groups provide valuable opportunities for social communication, but they lack a supervisor and facilitator who are trained in FRIEND®. With good communication between school personnel and parents, strategies from FRIEND can be extended to the student's home and community.

The parents' role in this process is indispensable because they:

- know their child better than anyone else

- provide a stable influence in their child's life

- are the most motivated individuals in their child's life

- have good ideas about what might work best for their child

- can teach and support new skills in many different settings

- can share in the enjoyment of activities with their child and cultivate that "shared enjoyment" with others.

At the same time, raising a child with social challenges is different than raising a typically developing child. Parents will benefit from learning and implementing the same interventions taught to their child's peers and school staff including modeling, prompting, shaping, offering choice, and providing appropriate praise and corrective feedback. There are also a few new strategies described in this chapter which parents can embed in their child's day. Of course, parents are busy with other children and work responsibilities so it's helpful to train in-home therapists and extended family members as well.

Extending teaching opportunities for a child with social challenges to a variety of settings is supported by meaningful research. It has long been understood that children with ASD have trouble generalizing new skills from therapy rooms to real-world environments. This difficulty is most likely due in part to a learning challenge in which the child with ASD attends to only part of the information presented when learning new skills. For example, a child with ASD may learn how to respond to another child in the speech therapist's office but not to the same child on the playground. This pattern of attention is called over-selectivity and is characterized by the impaired response to simultaneous multiple cues (Schreibman, 1988).

Even if a child doesn't struggle with ASD and over-selectivity, but instead is shy, anxious, or awkward, he or she will engage less than his or her more capable peers resulting in fewer opportunities to practice emerging social skills. Students who have trouble learning social skills and communication on their own benefit from direct teaching, but most importantly they need to practice these skills in as many different situations, and with as many different peers, as possible.

BEHAVIOR

Delays in the development of communication and socialization skills can lead to problem behavior. While poor communication skills may be the reason behind the development of maladaptive behaviors, parents can teach their child how to behave appropriately for his or her developmental level. By watching what is happening before their child engages in an inappropriate behavior, parents can learn what events might be difficult, or motivating, for their child and help correct the situation. Researchers have discovered that problem behaviors may occur for one or more of the following reasons:

- to avoid a task, interaction, or environment
- to gain attention
- to gain access to preferred items or activity
- to gain access to internal (intrinsic) reinforcement such as a preferred self-stimulatory activity.

As parents and therapists teach appropriate replacement skills such as initiating conversations, asking questions, and making relevant comments, inappropriate behaviors often decrease (Koegel and LaZebnik, 2004). A child who has overcome challenging behaviors will have more opportunities to participate in enriching family and community activities.

PLAY

Children learn while they are having fun. However, children with social challenges run the risk of being excluded from play or may avoid the social interactions that their peers enjoy. For those children who do want to play, social attempts can be immature or unconventional and off-putting to their peers (Kasari *et al.*, 2012).

The following strategies to teach play and social interactions are built on basic behavioral principles which make the process of teaching social skills less overwhelming. Some of the strategies are adapted from *Overcoming Autism* by Koegel and LaZebnik (2004). Once understood and mastered, these principles can be modified to be appropriate for a child of any age. A toddler or preschool-age child is probably spending lots of time inside the house playing with toys. An older child is learning how to share and take turns and will eventually play imaginative games with other children.

A school-age child may want to play sports, chat with friends, or play imaginative games with other children. Thus, skills that are taught should also vary according to the child's age and developmental level.

Regardless of the age of their child, parents can carefully observe what typical children do and determine how their child's behavior is different. Does their child play alone or next to other children? If he or she does try to interact, how do other kids respond? What kind of imaginary or active games are other kids playing? It's even important for parents to pay attention to what typical children are wearing, how their hair is cut, and what kind of lunchboxes they carry.

Parents can break down the skills their child needs to learn into small parts, so that they can teach play and social skills in a fun, motivating way. It's important that parents learn to be deliberate, patient, and confident that these interventions will work for their child.

Teach simple play at home

After observing their child at home to see what he or she likes to do, parents can choose toys, games, or activities that are age appropriate and motivating. Parents will want to make sure their child is relaxed, engaged, and having fun. If a new toy or game becomes a favorite for their child, parents may consider buying an extra one for school.

Since some children with ASD are inclined to play with toys repetitively (Wolfberg *et al.*, 2015), parents will need to ensure that their child plays with the new toy appropriately, even for a brief time, before letting him or her play the way he or she wants. Parents can motivate their child to play with new toys for longer and longer periods of time. Eventually, parents can hold off on the reward of allowing their child to play with the toy in the way he or she wants (often repetitively) until he or she plays appropriately with a sibling or peer.

Teach spontaneous play

Some children with social challenges may not gravitate to toys on their own. Parents can help their child learn how to play spontaneously by teaching him or her to look at and imitate what siblings, cousins, or neighbors are doing when playing on their own. Parents can focus their child's attention and scaffold their child's play by saying, for example, "Look, Sam's car is going to the store. Where is your car going?" Since some children with social challenges aren't naturally imitative (Wolfberg *et al.*, 2015), parents can teach their child to learn from the environment by saying, "What are the other kids doing?"

Teach pretend and symbolic play with others

The transition from simple play, where a child pushes a car on a pretend road, to symbolic play, where a child makes up a story about where the car is going and why, can be difficult for children with ASD (Williams, Reddy, and Costall, 2001).

Parents can entice children who don't have a lot of experience with pretend play by planning activities that are naturally motivating. For example, if their child loves animals, parents can take advantage of that interest and set up pretend play where everyone is going to the zoo or animals are the characters in a story.

Integrated Play Groups (IPGs) can help kids with social challenges develop imaginative and social play with friends who, like peers in FRIEND®, learn strategies to help their playmates (Wolfberg *et al.*, 2015). This intervention is based on the theory that play both mirrors and leads development. The term social constructivism suggests that social interaction plays a fundamental role in cognitive development. In other words, social learning precedes development. A mature playmate, parent, facilitator, or therapist can act as a teacher or coach for the child with social challenges. The zone of proximal development (ZPD) is the distance between a child's current independent play skills and what he or she is capable of under the guidance of a knowledgeable playmate or other "coach" (Vygotsky, 1978, p.86).

While IPGs were developed as an after-school program, the same strategies can be adapted by parents to use at home. In many respects an IPG functions like a FRIEND Lunch Group. An IPG is composed of a few "players" and one adult. The children meet where there are motivating games, materials, and activities that encourage joint attention, imitation, turn taking, and imaginary play. Examples of play materials might include beach or yoga balls for motor play, wooden blocks or LEGO™ for construction play, and a doctor kit or kitchen supplies for thematic play. Symbolic pretend play is one of the goals for children in these IPGs. This type of play is characterized by a child pretending to do something, or to be someone else. Play scripts vary with increasing complexity and cohesion between children over time. Examples of symbolic pretend play include:

- using one object to represent another such as holding a banana to the ear as if it were a telephone

- "pretending" to use something that isn't present such as holding a pretend light-saber or wizard's wand

- creating imaginary objects or events such as making an airplane noise while spreading out and moving the arms in the air

- role playing (real or invented) with dolls, self, peers, and/or imaginary characters such as a tea party with teddy bears, a telephone conversation with a make-believe person, or acting out a space fantasy with invented creatures.

Again, it's important that parents consider what is motivating for both their child and his or her playmates in the IPG. Each play "session" can include a greeting, fun presentation of the play materials, and about 40 minutes of guided participation in play, followed by clean-up, debrief, and good-byes (Wolfberg *et al.*, 2015). A hesitant or very shy child may need a reward to increase his or her play time with friends, and interactions may need to be short and relatively non-demanding while a child is developing confidence and skills.

Parents can use IPGs to observe how typical kids join an ongoing activity and then teach their child how to imitate his or her peers. The same is true for ending play. By encouraging their child to watch what typical kids say and do when leaving a group, parents can teach their child to say, "See you later," or "Could we finish the game later?" if he or she doesn't want to play anymore or is feeling overwhelmed.

IPGs also provide a great opportunity to teach good sportsmanship skills. Parents can teach kids in the group to cheer for the person who wins and say something like, "You did great." Kids can be acknowledged when they control their temper after losing a close game and be reminded that it's never "cool" to argue with another child or adult over points or how to play.

Parents might create IPGs that are based on seasons of the year or a child's special interests, or take requests from other players. To increase players' comfort and confidence when interacting with a child who has social challenges, parents can educate and support playmates by using strategies presented in Chapter 5 about the PSP. A brief conversation with players' parents can ensure that questions are answered and set the stage for cooperation. Of course, all participation should be voluntary, and will be if activities are fun and engaging. Always make "shared enjoyment" a goal.

The IPG model applies the core practices of guided participation, as shown in Table 8.1.

Table 8.1 The core practices of guided participation

Nurturing play
Parents recognize and respond to the subtle and unique ways their child expresses his or her interests and intentions to play with other children
Scaffolding play
Parents adjust the amount and type of support their child and playmates need to coordinate their play
Guiding social communication
Parents support their child and playmates in using words and gestures to get each other's attention, respond to each other, and stay engaged in play
Guiding play within the "zone of proximal development"
Parents use a continuum of strategies to engage their child when interacting with playmates in activities slightly beyond his or her capacity. Parents encourage their child to stay engaged, even if participation is minimal. For example: • Tom's car is getting gas. Where are you going on your trip?   • Peter is making a big fort. How are you guys making it safe from wild animals?   • Suzy is cooking spaghetti for dinner. What are you going to make?

Adapted from Wolfberg et al. (2015)

Cooperative play

Once a parent has taught their child how to join in with other children, take turns, and end play, he or she will still need many opportunities to practice these skills. As mentioned in Chapter 3, "Intervention Strategies," cooperative play can be an effective way to integrate and support children with social challenges in play with typical peers. Cooperative play is any organized recreation among children in which activities are planned for the purpose of achieving some goal. Some examples include a group art project, construction projects (e.g. building a fort), puzzles, putting on a play, or even board games.

Once the play is underway, the parent can continue to provide opportunities for children to interact by providing limited access to the components of the activity for the purpose of inspiring functional communication and encouraging the child with social challenges and playmates to talk about, request, and share materials. For example, if the kids are putting together a train track, the parent might separate the pieces into two bags so that the kids need to ask each other for the necessary pieces in order to complete the project. Table 8.2 gives some examples of cooperative play.

Table 8.2 Examples of cooperative play

Inside activities
• Bake cookies—each child can provide a different ingredient, or complete one aspect of the baking process
• Play charades
• Make a haunted house in the garage
• Make lunch together—one child spreads the peanut butter, another puts on the jelly
• Make ice-cream sundaes together
• Board games—checkers, chess
• Watch TV—use stuffed animals or action figures to pretend to be different characters
• Puzzles—each child has a few pieces
• Make a fort out of pillows—each child brings different supplies
• Card games—Crazy Eights, Slapjack, Old Maid, War
• Hangman
Crafts
• Design a collage together—one child draws the picture, one child provides the glue, another sprinkles the glitter
• Make a story book together
• Color pictures—divide up the crayons
• Magazine scavenger hunt
Outside
• Chase
• Hide and seek
• Freeze tag
• Plant a vegetable garden
• Play Marco-Polo in the swimming pool
At the park
• Treasure hunt
• Put on a circus show
• Duck, Duck, Goose

In the car
• Play I Spy
• Twenty Questions
• Word games

Adapted from Werner et al. (2006)

TEACH COMMUNICATION SKILLS
Younger children

Parents can promote communication skills in their young children by embedding naturally occurring language-enhancing strategies throughout their child's day (Moore *et al.*, 2013). Teaching communication and other functional skills at meaningful times increases learning opportunities and generalization. With very little effort, parents can teach a new skill without disrupting the flow of a fun, motivating activity. Using puppets, especially if they represent a special interest, can make practice sessions more like a game. In addition to playtime, parents can embed these strategies during caregiving routines, household chores, and community activities. Table 8.3 provides a few examples of where and when communication skills can be taught and practiced.

Table 8.3 Natural settings to teach communication

Indoor play	Outdoor play	Caregiving	Community activities
Car play	Swing	Hand washing	Mommy and Me classes
Stuffed animals and dolls	Slide	Mealtime	Gymnastics
Music	Riding tricycle	Bath	Library reading
Magna-Doodle	Riding bike	Dressing	Church services
Reading books	Catch	Brushing teeth	Pre-school
Blocks	Sidewalk chalk	Brushing hair	Swimming lessons
Piano	Wagon races	Putting toys away	Cooperative play with neighbors
Watching videos	Bubbles	Putting clothes away	
Peek-a-boo	Basketball	Feeding a pet	
Finger play	Chase		
	Sand play		

Adapted from Kaiser, Hancock, and Nietfeld (2000)

A family-centered approach will further increase learning opportunities and create a supportive atmosphere for parents, siblings, and extended family members. When parents are confident in their abilities, anxiety decreases and expectations for their child's success increases. Parent-focused interventions that occur throughout the day in natural settings have been found to decrease parental stress while resulting in greater gains in child communication (Koegel, Bimbela, and Schreibman, 1996).

Table 8.4 provides a description of language-enhancing strategies parents can use throughout their child's day.

Table 8.4 Language-enhancing strategies for parents

Language-enhancing strategy	Description
Wait and respond	Wait for child to communicate and then respond
Talk in short, simple sentences	When talking directly to your child, use sentences your child would be likely to say
Answer instead of asking	Avoid asking yes/no and "test" questions (for example: What color is this? How many do you have?)
Repeat and add	When your child says a sentence, repeat what he or she said and add a word or two
Do what your child does and talk about it	Imitate your child's action, and say what he or she would say
Say what your child would say	Respond to your child's spontaneous request/comments by saying the word/words your child might say in a way that encourages/prompts him or her to imitate you
Give your child a choice	Say the words for the items as you provide choices, such as, "Do you want milk or juice?"
Environmental arrangement	Give your child more opportunities to communicate by setting up situations where your child wants/needs to (For example: Ask for more of something, Seek your help, Comment on something new or silly)

Adapted from Moore, Barton, and Chironis (2014)

Older children

As a child gains communication skills there will be new strategies to learn and practice. In a conversation, the speaker and listener need to "get" each other's perspective to be effective partners. Without the ability to easily understand what someone else is thinking, children with ASD may talk endlessly about a topic that interests them, thinking that this topic interests their classmates and family as well. They fail to understand that their interests may bore or even irritate their peers (Ricks and Wing, 1975). Other challenges such as repetitive questions and statements, an inability to take turns, and difficulty in maintaining a topic can make conversational attempts frustrating for everyone. Children with ASD do not simply "outgrow" these deficits; rather these difficulties continue to negatively impact social and occupational functioning (Koegel and LaZebnik, 2004). Opportunities to improve conversation skills, not just language, become the focus for older children.

Parents can also have significant effects upon their child's relationships, both in terms of teaching and supervising new skills as well as supporting their child's development of an appropriate group of friends (Wood *et al.*, 2009). The Program for the Education and Enrichment of Relationship Skills (PEERS), a parent-assisted social skills group intervention for high-functioning adolescents with ASD, has been shown to be helpful in improving friendship skills (Laugeson *et al.*, 2012). While parents may not have access to this type of training in their community, there are several PEERS topics and strategies worth considering. Some of these topics have already been presented in the IPGs. As children master basic social interactions they need opportunities to learn and practice more complex skills independently.

Conversational skills

- Teach the child how to trade information during conversation with peers to find common interests.

- Instruct the child on elements of two-way conversation. The child will need to listen and respond to peers. This will take practice and perseverance for those kids who perseverate on preferred topics. As a child learns to listen it becomes easier to respond appropriately.

- Clarify what topics are appropriate and what topics are off limits. Social boundaries include topics of conversation.

- Just as parents observed how younger children enter play, parents of older children will need to teach their older child how to enter an ongoing conversation. Parents can teach their child to listen and when appropriate, give their opinion or ask a question. If one child doesn't know what a peer is talking about, but it sounds interesting, they may ask about it. However, asking people what they're talking about can sometimes be annoying if a child isn't part of a social group. Kids with social challenges need to learn about these boundaries so they don't butt into any conversation. It is often best to start with a small comment and judge the reaction before continuing, ensuring they don't cut someone off when making a new comment.

- Parents can teach their child how to exit or end a conversation as well. Even the best conversations will eventually run out of steam or be ended by an interruption. The child should smile, state they enjoyed the conversation, and say goodbye. Ending on a positive note will make the other person want to talk to the teen again.[1]

Electronic media

Parents will want to teach their child about how to use voicemail, email, text messaging, instant messaging, and the internet in developing friendships. Social media can be an effective tool to extend a child with social challenges social opportunities, but only if they are used appropriately.

Basic online rules include:

- Real people take priority (family and friends are more important than playing with a cell phone).

- If you wouldn't say it to someone's face, don't say it online.

- If you wouldn't show it in public, don't share it online.

- Don't exclude your audience (don't post an obscure comment to your Facebook status, list serve, or forum).

- Don't "friend" then "unfriend" people.

- Respect people's privacy.

- Don't repost without checking the facts.

- Check and respond to email promptly.

- Update online information that people depend on.[2]

---

1   See Wikihow.com/Have-a-Great-Conversation
2   See Ten Rules of Netiquette at http://addictions.about.com/od/internetaddiction/tp/Ten-Rules-Of-Netiquette.htm

HANDLING TEASING AND DISAGREEMENTS

It's inevitable that children with social challenges will occasionally be teased. Providing strategies for dealing with teasing ahead of time will ensure that kids know what to do during those stressful moments and can also re-frame their thinking to preserve self-esteem. Of course, it's important that parents ensure that their child doesn't take out his or her frustration and anger on other kids.

Helpful strategies include:

- Shrug and walk away.

- Ignore the teasing.

- Self-talk:

  - "I don't like this but I can handle this."

  - "I don't believe what this kid is saying about me."

  - "I have a lot of strengths."

- Visualization:

  - Child pictures him- or herself as a ball and the words that the teaser is saying are bouncing off.

  - Child pretends there is a bubble around him or her so the words can't get through.

  - Child imagines him- or herself as a super-power figure who is safe from put downs.

- Positive thinking:

  - Child has the power to choose how to act when someone is teasing.

  - Child can decide that he or she doesn't have to let the other person have power.

  - The person who has the power is the one who stays in control.[3]

---

3 Adapted from https://www.counseling.org/resources/library/selected%20 Topics/Bullying/Teasing.htm

Conflict is unavoidable at times. Children with social challenges have things that are important to them, feelings that overwhelm them, and beliefs they are passionate about. These strategies can help:

- All feelings are OK.

- Separate feelings about what someone is doing from your feelings about the person.

- Practice empathy (try to see things from the other person's point of view) before approaching a conflict.

- It can be less important to "win" and more important to maintain a relationship with a friend or sibling.

- If you need to calm down, walk away.

- Listen as well as talk.

- When arguments break out, make it a teachable moment. In addition to giving a child a consequence, teach him or her how to improve his or her behavior in the future.

- Try to see the other person as being on the same side.[4]

CORRECTIVE FEEDBACK

When providing feedback, it's important to remember that individuals with social challenges can be overwhelmed, especially when they are learning many new skills. Appropriate use of corrective feedback can help maintain motivation. Feedback should be specific, frequent, contingent on a child's behavior, and varied. Another helpful strategy is to embed a suggestion between two compliments. For example, a parent might say, "I liked the way you stayed cool when Tyler won at Scrabble. Next time you might say, 'great game.' You're a good sport, Alex." Another example would be, "It was great you called Cole. What does he like to talk about? You're becoming a good listener, Briggs." Everyone tries harder when they feel successful or know how they can be.

---

4   See www.disabled-world.com/health/neurology/autism/conflicts.php

INTEGRATE AND SUPPORT THE CHILD IN THE COMMUNITY

When Sean was diagnosed with autism we were lucky to find specialists who focused on inclusion models. They told us to involve Sean in community and school activities right away and never hold him back because of autism. We took that recommendation seriously. Every year we hosted birthday parties for Sean and invited all the kids in the neighborhood. We took Sean to swimming lessons, and signed him up for Taekwondo, soccer, and a summer pottery class. When he was in sixth grade, he auditioned and was accepted into a community children's choir. There were some activities that Sean liked and others he didn't. We eventually dropped the soccer and pottery classes and encouraged swimming, scouts, and his community choir. Being involved in these activities didn't cure his autism, but they made his life richer. We knew what we had to do for Sean, but the rest of the world didn't understand autism the way we did. We needed to support him and help others support him too. When he went to camp I volunteered to be camp nurse. When he went to Europe as part of the touring choir, his dad volunteered to be a chaperone. Looking back, if we didn't have a child with autism we probably wouldn't have been as involved in these activities. Not only were we making Sean's life richer, we were enriching our lives too. Having a child with ASD made us into better, more active parents.

When parents thoughtfully integrate their child with social challenges into the community, he or she will have meaningful opportunities to improve their communication, manage relationships, solve problems flexibly, and learn to regulate their emotions. While FRIEND® works to improve social and communication skills directly, it is unique in its efforts to improve the wider school and community context for children and youth with social challenges.

Parents can use the child's interests, such as music, scouts, art, swimming, or chess, to determine community activities their child might want to participate in. Strategies used in Chapter 5 about the PSP can be adapted when parents educate a scout group or community choir. Leaders and peers develop confidence in their ability to support and befriend a child with social challenges when they have the information and strategies to be successful. Community activities provide the structure and ongoing opportunities to build meaningful relationships. With encouragement from parents, children with social challenges can learn how to invite a few like-minded peers over for a movie and pizza.

> As a person with autism, I directly benefitted from organized social interactions. For my Eagle Scout project, I helped organize a choir group and we called ourselves Rhythm 'N' Song. My music therapist helped lead and structure the group activities. The goal was to provide a social experience involving music for kids with autism and friends from my scout and church youth group. I selected some of my favorite songs, including "This Land is Your Land" and "Yankee Doodle Joy," and bought kazoos for the kids. We all hung out together during the four practices and before the performance. In the beginning we played games to get to know each other a little better and then practiced singing for the next hour. In one game I liked we each created a rhythm to do before we said our name. Everyone had to remember the rhythm and say the name that went along with it. This game helped me to pay attention to what other kids were doing and learn their name. At other times we practiced with chimes and drums and we discovered that one of the kids with autism who was non-verbal had a great time playing the drums. At the last meeting we performed for 40 of our family and friends. We sang "This Land is Your Land," "Yankee Doodle Joy," and "Hedwig's Theme" from *Harry Potter and the Sorcerer's Stone*. We all really liked that one.

FRIENDLY COMMUNICATION (BETWEEN PARENTS AND EDUCATORS)

One of the benefits of parents and school staff working together is the opportunity for communication about the student with challenges in a timely and helpful manner. An effective way to communicate on a consistent basis is with a communication binder in which parents and teachers share information with each other regularly. The binder helps to avoid surprises in the future.

A communication binder can be set up with the following sections:

- team members with contact information

- schedule

- current goals

- description of intervention strategies to be used by parents, peer participants, and school staff to ensure consistency

- summary of data
  - what's working
  - what needs to be modified

- communication section

- ideas for social skill-building activities at home

- games, social activities, and topics enjoyed by peer participants

- games, social activities, and topics enjoyed by the child with ASD

- questions, challenges, success stories, new ideas

- a roster of names, addresses, and phone numbers to foster social opportunities outside of school, if acceptable to the peer participants and their parents.

As the most motivated member of the staff–parent working team, it is often the parent that provides the energy and impetus to ensure consistency from year to year, especially when the child transitions from elementary to middle school, and from middle to high school. Consistency can ensure that no time is lost at the beginning of the school year in setting up a FRIEND® Lunch Group.

WHAT INDIVIDUALS WITH CHALLENGES NEED MOST

Our son, Tony, has autism and has always worked hard to be independent. In high school he rode his bike to school every day. One day a group of students drove past Tony and threw an open can of soda at him. He was soaked but continued to school and never told us. Fortunately, our neighbor witnessed the incident and quickly jotted down their license plate number. She reported the incident to the Principal who called the guilty students into his office. They admitted throwing the can at Tony, but claimed it was an accident. They were innocently "cleaning out their car" when Tony was struck by the soda can. They wrote a letter of apology to Tony, who takes things at face value, so he believed that the incident was not meant to be malicious.

We wouldn't have known about the event if our neighbor hadn't told us what had happened a few days later. The episode reminded us when you have a child with autism, it's important that you create a community of support among neighbors, extended family, school, and religious community. The strategies outlined in the FRIEND Program helped us create that for Tony.

Overcoming challenges, however we define it, cannot be done alone. Each individual's progress will be influenced by everyone around him or her. Ensure the parent is aware of the following:

- Each child needs his or her family, therapists, and educators to treat him or her as though he or she will be successful.

- Regardless of whether it will take two years, twenty years, or a lifetime, each child needs people around him or her who have faith in his or her ability to continue to learn and grow.

- Each child needs a family who loves him or her for who he or she is and the person he or she will become.

- Trust that your child is trying, although perhaps not at your skill level or on your schedule.

- Speak directly to your child, not about him or her to others.

- Focus development in areas of interest and competence for your child.

- Look for ways to improve your child's quality of life, and yours too.

- Develop shared enjoyment with your child's activities and interests.

- Celebrate all of your child's successes.

- Tell your family and friends about your child's challenges so they can offer their support.

- Keep your family informed about your child's progress and ask them to do specific things to support you.

- Be protective of your child, but don't stand in the way of his or her progress.

Refer to the section titled "Tips for Parents" for ideas and strategies to help your child learn and practice social skills every day at home and in the community (Appendix V).

CHAPTER SUMMARY

✓ With good communication between school personnel and parents, this program can be extended to the student's home, neighborhood, scout groups, and community activities.

✓ Over-selectivity may prevent a student with social challenges from attending to the multiple cues presented in a learning situation. This can prevent generalization of new skills.

✓ Parents are in the best position to help their child with social challenges generalize play and social skills by using language-enhancing strategies and incidental teaching to teach communication during indoor and outdoor play, chores, dressing, snacks, and meals.

✓ Parents can help their child learn how to play with toys, imitate, and play imaginative games with peers in IPGs by nurturing and scaffolding play, encouraging social communication, and guiding play with a more experienced playmate (especially symbolic and imaginative play).

✓ Parents can improve the larger social context for children with social challenges by extending FRIEND® strategies into local schools and the larger community.

✓ Parents can encourage the use of a communication binder between the school and home to improve the effectiveness of the FLP.

✓ Parents can join the school team in celebrating their child's successes in the FRIEND program and encourage continuity from year to year.

9

Conclusion

BE FLEXIBLE

FRIEND® is a comprehensive social skill program implemented in typical settings with peers and age-appropriate activities. Essentially, FRIEND encourages school-wide and small group PBS to assist in the development of social communication and play skills of students with social challenges. As peers learn to provide support, they can become more tolerant and supportive friends, and eventually, adults. FRIEND becomes part of the school culture, and the impact can be life changing for all students.

OVERCOMING CHALLENGES TO THE PROGRAM

Schools may hesitate to engage in FRIEND because of staff requirements. It is essential that the Lunch Program and Playground Program have a supervisor and facilitator. When the student has an aide, it is somewhat easier because the aide can be trained to fulfill the facilitator role. In some situations, the aide may be capable of supporting more than one student with social challenges. If the student does not have an aide, skilled playground or lunchroom staff can be helpful. This decreases the burden on the school to hire additional staff or consultants to implement the program. However, if they need to continuously monitor a number of students, their attention may be too divided for successful implementation. Whether an aide or staff member is the facilitator, all staff in the lunchroom or playground need to be aware of FRIEND and its procedures so they can help support the program.

As facilitators need supervisors, identifying professionals with leadership and clinical skills is another challenge. Again, reorganizing existing staff schedules and responsibilities can help without adding additional burden. For example, the school psychologist who typically sees a student weekly can observe him or her on the playground instead of in his or her office. A speech and language pathologist who sees a given student for 30 minutes per week can use speech time to teach facilitators how to implement the student's social and communication goals at lunchtime. The special education teacher who has allotted time with each student weekly can use some of that time to supervise the facilitators. Staffing FRIEND® will require flexibility and patience. However, once the staff become aware of the importance (and benefits) of addressing social challenges during recess or lunch, they will likely have increased motivation to find the time.

Teaching social skills is a blend of science and art. There is no better place to learn these skills than at school. Special education teachers, school psychologists, speech therapists, teachers, and classroom aides are professionals who dedicate their careers to helping children in need. Adapting their schedules to implement an effective program may be easier than it appears.

The following case studies illustrate the benefits of the program from several perspectives.

CASE STUDIES

Cory

When our son, Cory, was in middle school he wanted friends. However, he usually talked about his favorite subjects over and over which included computers, languages, jokes from Garrison Keillor's *Pretty Good Joke Book*, geography, politics, world religion, and cars. When his dad and I had a chance to see him at school, he was usually standing too close to his classmates asking the same questions over and over. Cory had a very capable school aide assisting him for part of the day. We could tell she was trying to help Cory with prompts and suggestions, but after a while they were both frustrated and he was still acting odd around his classmates. Eventually most of the kids just ignored him. He was becoming even more anxious and frustrated around the kids he wanted to talk to and was irritable and unhappy at home. His teachers reported that he was having trouble concentrating in class too.

We'd heard about FRIEND® from the Southwest Autism Research & Resource Center and were desperate to find something to help Cory. We bought two manuals, one for the middle school's IEP team and one for us to keep at home. Next we called an IEP meeting. It took a while for the team to understand how the program might work. They were concerned about involving Cory's typical classmates. Without any experience with FRIEND, they weren't confident that peers could be taught to support Cory. However, like Cory's school aide, the team understood that it was necessary to help him feel more comfortable and confident around his classmates.

The IEP team reviewed the FRIEND manual. The speech therapist, who was initially skeptical about working on social pragmatics, called Southwest Autism Research & Resource Center (SARRC) and got some practical advice about how to get started. We offered to help coordinate the program and buy pizza for the FRIEND meeting that was scheduled every two weeks. The speech therapist realized that she could use her therapy time for Cory as a coordinator of the program.

The team met and decided to go forward with FRIEND and added several social skill goals to Cory's IEP:

1. Cory would eat lunch with and talk with typical kids 80 percent of the time at lunch.

2. Cory would improve his pragmatic conversational skills by responding to, and building on, his friends' topics of interest 80 percent of the time.

3. Cory would improve his eye contact by looking at his peers during conversations 80 percent of the time.

At home we talked with Cory about who he might want to eat with at lunch. The school team also thought about which kids might be interested in participating in the program. Three adolescent boys, who were already friends and shared several classes with Cory, were invited to join FRIEND. The team used permission letters in the back of the manual to educate the parents of the typical kids about FRIEND®. It was clear that participation was voluntary and FRIEND never took time away from academic programming. We were thrilled when all three of the kids identified by the IEP team decided to participate. Parents were pleased that their kids were selected to participate because of their leadership skills, kindness, and maturity. The speech therapist spent time with the kids explaining the program and determined that they all wanted to participate. She also spent time with Cory, away from the other kids, describing how the program would work. Cory was both nervous and excited about starting FRIEND. The speech therapist and Cory's aide spent time with the FRIEND group at lunch, helping them get acquainted and feel comfortable with one another. They occasionally prompted the kids to include Cory in all their conversations.

The group decided to meet every day for lunch at a particular place in the cafeteria. The FRIEND participants were given an early lunch pass so they could get through the cafeteria line early, allowing more time for them to be together at lunch. Once the typical kids understood the strategies to help Cory, they were confident about what to do and enjoyed spending time with him. Cory was able to practice social communication skills in a natural setting, every day at lunch and throughout the school day. We found that he was much more motivated to learn social skills from kids his age instead of us or even his speech therapist. The team reported that Cory's new friends spent time with him between classes, and sometimes before and after school.

Every two weeks, we called in an order for pizza and soda for the group (we even started to get discounts from the restaurant). The FRIEND Group met in the speech therapist's office and discussed what was going well with the group and what needed to be improved. Sometimes they had questions or needed new ideas about how to help Cory. The kids decided how they wanted to spend their time together during these group meetings. The meetings were fun, too. They played games like charades or Twenty Questions in the classroom. The kids always included some games that Cory especially enjoyed.

Both the aide and speech therapist would meet with the Lunch Group occasionally during the week, just to make sure everything was going well. Sometimes the group would come up with ideas about how to help Cory. For example, Cory had the off habit of picking up, and eating, pieces of salt from the table that had dropped off his soft-pretzel. This seemed sort of weird to the kids so they suggested that he eat only the salt that landed on his paper plate. Once he did that, the group was more comfortable with him during lunch.

We met with the school team every eight weeks to discuss how the program was working. It was great to hear that Cory was feeling more comfortable at school and he was doing better in his classes, too. We often came up with ideas about how to improve the program at school, but we also learned some things we could do at home to support FRIEND®. For example, we learned from the aide that most kids were talking about a new cartoon on TV. We started watching the show at home so Cory could share in the conversations with the other kids. This gave him another appropriate topic to discuss at school.

FRIEND easily spread to other areas of Cory's life. We invited the FRIEND participants over for Cory's birthday party, and many times he invited them over to play video games. We also introduced FRIEND strategies to Cory's scout troop and community choir. It was great for us to see Cory with his friends in many different settings. We were amazed and thrilled that the group stayed together all three years in middle school. Cory's social skills improved and he was much less irritable at home. Surprisingly the speech therapist reported that the typical kids' social and communication skills improved as well. They remarked that it was one of the best parts of their school day.

Summary

In this case study, FRIEND was in its early development. The goals that were decided for Cory were not based on any type of quantitative assessment of his skills. As the program developed we have recognized the need for careful and structured development and implementation. Impairments may often seem obvious, but if wrong goals are developed then the program could be wasting time and resources. The assessments we recommend in this manual will help make data-driven decisions and help to ensure the efficient and successful implementation of the program.

Jake

Our son, Jake, was diagnosed with Asperger's Syndrome (AS) when he was eight years old, about the same time he started playing chess. He was a gifted student with strong skills in many areas. Since the school didn't have much experience working with kids with AS, Jake had a really rough time in elementary school. He didn't have any real friends back then. He was anxious around other kids and generally just left them alone. Eventually, other kids stopped trying to hang out with him, and some of them bullied Jake.

The saddest and most difficult time for Jake was between 13 and 15. He really wanted friends, but didn't know how to act around the other kids. Jake also talked in a loud, sort of pedantic voice, like a teacher. He avoided eye contact and interrupted other kids. He stood too close when he talked and tried to steer the conversation to his favorite topics. That wouldn't have been so bad except his interests were so limited: chess, politics, and superheroes. He was opinionated and had trouble when other kids disagreed with him. He was teased a lot in PE. He wasn't very coordinated and got suspended at the end of eighth grade when he shoved someone. He was angry when none of his tormentors got into trouble.

By the time Jake was in high school he was really anxious and depressed. We'd heard about FRIEND® from another parent and felt that some of the strategies would help Jake so we went on SARRC's website and ordered a FRIEND manual. Then we met with the IEP team. Fortunately, there was already a culture of acceptance and inclusiveness at the school and a strict no-bullying policy. The team had been working with some other kids with AS so they had some ideas about how to help Jake.

We completed some assessments and the team observed Jake at lunch and PE before our next planning meeting. The team spent a lot of time talking about Jake's skills. He has a really good vocabulary, an amazing deep voice, and is especially good at science and chess. Jake knows he has AS but he didn't want any of the other kids knowing about his diagnosis. With some persuasion, Jake was willing to join the chess club that met once a week after school, but he was still eating alone every day. Mr. Fagrell, who supervised the chess club, could tell that Jake was having a really tough time with the other kids. It's hard for anyone who knows Jake to understand how he can be gifted and have so many social problems.

Jake was emotionally immature. He had never learned to be a gracious loser; he would lose his temper if the game didn't go his way. Mr. Fagrell saw this as a big problem for Jake and wanted to help. He opened his classroom at lunchtime so the team could hang out, eat, and play chess. He wanted the team to have more playing time anyway. The group was supervised, with clear expectations about behavior, so generally everyone got along well. I think it helped that Mr. Fagrell had a nephew with Asperger's Syndrome so he was really comfortable giving Jake clear behavior limits but also the encouragement to keep trying something that was hard for him. With the extra practice during these lunch meetings, Jake became a better sport. As another benefit to the program, Jake started to pay attention to what the other kids were eating. Before, he only wanted peanut butter and jelly for lunch every day then his friends started commenting. Eventually, he listened to them and included more foods that his friends were eating.

The speech therapist, Ms. Simpson, suggested Jake take a drama class since he had a great voice and excellent memory. Since a lot of the kids in drama tended to be a little different, Jake felt pretty comfortable around them. I'm sure the kids knew there was something odd about Jake but they accepted him and maybe even appreciated some of his idiosyncrasies. Ms. Simpson was able to meet with a few of the kids separately, telling them that Jake was shy, and she suggested some strategies they could use to help him fit in. Since Jake was able to practice social skills in a more comfortable setting, and throughout the school day, he was able to improve his eye contact and became less compulsive in his conversations.

The IEP team met every two months discussing how things were going and what we could do better. Although the school required PE, we were able to persuade them to drop that requirement for Jake since we'd provided evidence that our family had joined the YMCA. That meant that Jake had a free period. He was able to go to his homeroom every day where he could get a start on his homework and make sure he was organized and ready for the next day. This meant a lot less stress at home. Once Jake's team started seeing his improvement it was easier for each of us to think of something we could do better.

As a family, we worked on some strategies as well:

- We taught Jake to have an assertive and honest response when he was being teased.

- We invited some kids from the chess and drama club to hang out with Jake on the weekend.

- We made sure that Jake got some exercise every day.

- Since Jake was less depressed, it was easier for him to work on his personal hygiene.

- We recruited Jake's siblings to introduce him to current trends in music, movies, and fashion.

Now at the end of the school year, Jake has a few kids who genuinely like him, quirks and all. He's not dreading tenth grade, as he was his freshman year. His increased quality of life has been worth all the efforts we've put into making FRIEND® work for him. For Jake, it has never been a formal program, but rather an informal network of individuals who work together creating social supports and opportunities for him. We've discovered that he's even felt comfortable enough with some of his classmates to tell them about his diagnosis. Given the number of kids with challenges like Jake, he was surprised to hear that a lot of his friends had family members or neighbors with ASD. He's feeling less alone.

Summary

FRIEND can be as simple as having students with social challenges participate in existing school programs that align with their interests. Depending on the skills of the student, it may not need to be a major reorganization of the school day. This scenario is more common once students are in high school, when there is no recess period. Regardless, a key element is identifying motivated and tolerant peers to help support the individual. Sometimes peers need minimal guidance to see through the differences of another student, and identify the similarities that lead to friendship. Effect on peers is just one of the many possible collateral benefits of FRIEND®. Another might be encouragement to eat a healthier diet and live a healthier lifestyle. For some students, change occurs with the motivation to be like other students who are their friends.

Sam

Two months into the school year a new student joined my second grade class. Sam was a boy with autism who didn't talk much. His IEP team wanted him placed in a classroom with typical peers and a full-time aide for a few classes every day. When Sam does talk, he repeats things other people say, or things from TV. Judging from the phrases we heard, superhero cartoons were clearly his favorite. Sam also loves music. In fact, he loves music so much I had to lock up the DVD player because when he sees it I can't get him to do anything else.

Although Sam has a full-time aide who works very hard at helping him, she too struggles and we both feel she spends most of her time following him around to make sure he is safe and doesn't interfere with the other students' learning.

During lunch Sam sits with his aide. It's always Sam and his aide. During recess I can always find Sam walking by himself on the playground. He will sit on the swing if his aide pushes him but other than that he just wanders aimlessly around. There is such a huge gap in Sam's social abilities as compared with his classmates. I realized we needed to do something different.

I immersed myself in reading everything I could about autism. I found it very interesting that our focus for Sam was on academic and self-help skills. If social skill development is a core deficit of autism and qualifies an individual for a diagnosis, then why wasn't Sam's IEP team focused more on his social skills? The more I learned, the more I understood we needed to find a different way to help Sam. We needed to use the aide's time more effectively to help Sam have a better experience at school.

I met a teacher from another school district who told me about FRIEND. She explained her school was implementing this program throughout her entire district. After listening to her talk about this program I realized we could offer a FRIEND program for Sam. My principal gave me permission to visit this teacher's school with Sam's mother.

The following week I invited Sam's mother and our principal to meet with the IEP team and discuss FRIEND®. Everyone was excited and the team discussed how they could support the program. After a period of observation and assessments, Sam's speech therapist changed her schedule around so she could facilitate the group at lunch as well as train his aide so she too could support the group during recess and throughout the school day. I teamed up with Sam's mother to provide a peer sensitivity training to the class. The wheels were in motion. Our team was thrilled we could offer a program that provided Sam with the opportunity to develop social skills and have a truly inclusive experience.

Before we could get started we needed to carefully select peers. We discussed many different students and what they could bring to the program, but we had a problem creating a cohesive group. I noticed a group of three boys that always hung around together before school, at lunch, and at recess. They were always playing pretend superhero games. They took turns being different characters. They weren't very popular kids, but they also weren't picked on by others. I asked them if they would be interested in learning more about Sam and trying to play with him sometimes. I knew he liked superheroes so I thought he would fit right in; they agreed and we had our FRIEND group. The parents of the kids invited to join the FRIEND group were pleased to give their permission.

The next step was to meet with the group to get their input on planning for the group. The kids were excited because they felt part of something fun. By the end of our first meeting we had a list of activities for the bi-monthly Friday pizza lunch and had discussed Sam's challenges, shared strategies to support him, and made a plan that the kids could go to the speech therapist if they had any questions.

The students ate lunch together almost every day. One of the boys started to sit next to Sam during music class and used the same strategies he learned in the FRIEND group during music. On rainy days the music teacher let some of the students hang out in the music room. Sam started going with this boy to the music room too. I noticed the kids in the FRIEND group helped Sam during class time too.

Summary

Not every child will benefit from FRIEND® in the same way. In the ideal situation, all students with challenges who participate in FRIEND will have near typical social functioning going forward. While the intent of the program is to build social skills in an individual with social challenges, some may not meet the ideal goal of near typical functioning; a student's limitations may prevent that from happening. Regardless, the student's general functioning will likely improve if they are happier in a given environment, especially at school where there can be so many rich social opportunities for students to enjoy and learn from.

Alexa

As a four-year-old child diagnosed with ASD, Alexa attended a special needs preschool program. She rode the bus to a school in her district far beyond the boundaries of her immediate neighborhood. Alexa made the long bus ride to this particular school because it offered her a classroom experience with a stellar teacher and staff that understood her needs. Each day after school Alexa either attended private therapy or participated in hours of an intensive behavioral home therapy program. From the beginning to the end of Alexa's day, she was engaged in evidence-based interventions. Her daily schedule of therapies required her to be surrounded by adults, which limited her opportunities for peer interactions.

Alexa's parents tried to encourage friendships with other children by inviting them over to the house. Alexa's parents provided many fun activities and yummy food they knew the other kids would enjoy, but they didn't think these gatherings were very successful. The kids had fun but ignored Alexa, and she always avoided them. Alexa's parents were frustrated and disappointed with their attempts to create social opportunities for their daughter.

Alexa's parents heard about FRIEND and decided to learn more. After some reading, they met with their IEP team and introduced the program. The team agreed the program should be implemented to support Alexa in developing social relationships with her peers. Adequate time for assessments and planning helped the team identify goals and objectives. They defined how each person's role, as specified on the IEP, could be utilized for successful FRIEND® program implementation. The speech therapist and Alexa's mother collaborated in providing a peer sensitivity training for the class. All the children's parents were invited to attend, as well as the principal, vice principal, bus driver, and school nurse. The speech therapist took Alexa out of the class for speech therapy during the peer sensitivity training. Together, Alexa's mother and teacher explained autism to the group. They showed a film and played a game that helped illustrate how to be a friend to a student with challenges.

The mother copied the "Tips for Peers" from the FRIEND manual for the parents of the other children. She made copies of the "Tips for Teachers" and gave them to every adult working with Alexa. She then shared the "Tips for Parents" with her husband and together they carefully discussed how to make use of FRIEND at home.

The paraprofessional knew Alexa liked to chase a ball, color with sidewalk chalk, and play in the sand. She also knew kids who liked to do the same things and asked them to be in the FRIEND group. She created cooperative arrangements always using one of these activities to facilitate peer interactions. The goal for each activity was always to increase initiations and response to peers during recess. Shortly after FRIEND started at school, Alexa's mother contacted moms of the kids in FRIEND to invite them over for play dates. Each play date was scheduled for one hour of carefully planned fun activities to help keep the kids engaged. She was so happy to plan a successful play date rather than anguish over the previous failed attempts.

Summary

An individual student's FRIEND program is best developed and implemented at school where peers and professionals can help support the student with social challenges. Students learn social skills best from a variety of settings. It is unrealistic to assume that students will only need support at school. A more comprehensive support program will be created if FRIEND strategies are implemented in other environments too. Parents should be active members of the FRIEND team and teach others (scouts, soccer teams, clubs, and neighbors) to implement the same strategies.

There is tremendous benefit from using FRIEND® to add structure to play dates at home so they are fun and successful learning opportunities.

Xavier

I work as a speech therapist in a middle school and have a caseload of 50 students who are served under Individuals with Disabilities Education Act (IDEA) in all categories. My school week is spent providing individual, small group, and consultation services to students as determined in their IEP. Of the 50 students, 20 have an ASD diagnosis. As is common with ASD, each student has individual strengths and challenges. However, social communication support is a common need among all of my students.

I searched through lots of resource material for evidence-based interventions that I could use with all of my students but one that was appropriate for everyone was hard to find. Then a colleague gave me the FRIEND manual. While reading, I discovered this was a program I could implement with each of my students to address their individual needs.

Initially this was an overwhelming task as it meant I would need to start 20 FRIEND groups (one for each student on my caseload). However, I was already attending IEP meetings for each student, providing direct or indirect services and documenting progress on IEP goals for each of them. I started with one student first, Xavier, who had an IEP meeting coming up anyway. The materials provided in FRIEND helped focus our IEP meeting and team. Xavier was diagnosed with Asperger's Syndrome. He was at or above grade level with all of his academics, but struggled socially. Using the observation tool in FRIEND, as well as an assessment of social pragmatics, it was easy to see why. His parents indicated that Xavier had no friends and sometimes came home talking about jokes and insults he'd heard at his expense. They said he spent his afternoons finishing his homework, and then playing games on the computer.

Xavier, as well as his parents, was involved in a planning meeting after our team had completed our initial assessments. He was curious about the program but also nervous about sharing his diagnosis with his classmates. The biggest concern was that the kids would have one more thing to tease him about. I explained that some of the research indicates that if students are given correct information, as well as strategies to interact, the teasing would decrease.

The team was on board and ready to begin. I worked with his parents to plan an appropriate peer sensitivity training for Xavier's science class. The school psychologist presented the peer sensitivity training, with Xavier's parents in attendance. The students were interested in learning about Asperger's Syndrome and how they could help Xavier feel more included at school. Before their first meeting I met with the identified peer participants as a group and provided them with "Tips for Peers," as well as some specific strategies to help Xavier meet some of his social goals. We agreed to meet again in a month to touch base and see how Xavier was progressing. I also met with Xavier individually during our allotted therapy time to discuss the group and his goals. He was excited to have kids willing to eat lunch with him at school for the first time.

After two weeks, Xavier's parents called to tell me about an instance during lunch when some kids starting teasing Xavier, but his new friends stood up for him and helped him leave the situation. He had never been able to do that before. I used my allotted service time to meet with the FRIEND® group regularly so we could talk about successes and problem solve through some of our greatest challenges.

Once this group was going, I had two more students with IEPs coming up. I decided to implement FRIEND for them, using my time as determined in their IEPs. After six months, I had started ten FRIEND groups, with each new one a little easier to start. I found that the school psychologist, principal, vice principal, and special education teacher were on many of the same IEP teams. Since they were willing to support this program school wide, we were able to work together to support each group as needed.

CHAPTER SUMMARY

✓ After taking the time to learn the principles and strategies of FRIEND® you will see it can be implemented with relative ease.

✓ FRIEND focuses on adding support to unstructured times of the school day (and in other settings) to benefit students who otherwise would have few opportunities to learn and practice social skills.

✓ It does not require new or extra staff to implement on an ongoing basis, but rather the commitment from staff and professionals who are there to support the student anyway.

✓ It is a matter of recognizing the need to support and learning the strategies to support in a meaningful way.

✓ All programs are better when a school adopts its principles as part of its culture.

✓ When an entire school is more tolerant, accepting and providing PBS to all students, everyone comes out ahead.

Appendix I: Introductory Documents

FRIEND® is a program that can be started by parents, professionals, or school staff. The documents in this appendix can help the person who is starting the program introduce it to the school, the parents, and peers. All of these forms can also be downloaded from www.jkp.com/voucher using the code NEYSOJY.

✓

Letter of introduction to school staff

To Whom It May Concern,

Thank you for your interest in FRIEND®: Fostering Relationships in Early Network Development. FRIEND is an intervention program designed to support the development of friendships between a student with social challenges and their peer community.

Creating a program is simple and cost effective because the resources are already available in your school. Staffing is determined by the support services and goals, which are already identified on the student's Individual Education Plan. Getting started involves the following:

1. *Schedule a meeting:* Invite key members at the school (i.e. teacher, principal, and psychologist) or the IEP team (if the student has one).

2. *Commitment:* Establish a common agreement among the student's IEP team to implement FRIEND.

3. *Responsibility:* Identify key team members to staff the program. Because this program is based on social communication skills and emotional development, it is recommended a speech therapist be directly involved. In addition to at least one of the student's parents, other staff participants should be determined according to the IEP, such as paraprofessional support, therapists, social worker, or school psychologist.

4. *Organization:* Any of the above listed people can organize or coordinate the program. Identify who will do what. Refer to the manual on how to organize a FRIEND group.

5. *Identify a start date:* The manual describes the process for identifying and establishing the typical peer group participants and getting started.

Thanks again for helping make a difference in the life of a child with social challenges and in the lives of their peers.

Sincerely,
(Your name)
(Your title)

FRIEND® permission slip

From a typical peer's perspective, FRIEND® is nothing more than engaging in structured play activities and helping a classmate. However, before they enroll, it is helpful to obtain consent from their parents. By doing so, you also make the parents aware of the program and they may help support it by reinforcing the efforts of the peers when they are home. Additionally, it is an easy way to share contact information with parents so they can call and ask questions if necessary.

Dear Parents,

We are excited to announce FRIEND®, a program to enhance social development for students by increasing opportunities to learn and practice social skills in a supportive environment. Many students have challenges interacting with others that impact their ability to be part of the school community.

In FRIEND, a small group of classmates and a peer with social differences will eat lunch together at school. A trained social facilitator supports the group so all students are engaged in appropriate activities that promote interaction. It may even extend to the playground during recess.

FRIEND includes the following components. Any of the following may be implemented at your child's school.

- Peer Sensitivity Training

  - Impacts awareness and understanding of differences observed in classmates.

  - Offers strategies for appropriate interaction with students who have challenges.

- FRIEND Lunch Program

  - Provides structure for a student with challenges and a small group of typical peers.

  - Implemented during lunch in the cafeteria (or a classroom) to support opportunities to learn and practice social communication skills.

✓

- FRIEND® Playground Program (for elementary age students)

  – Structured and supervised play activities during recess.

  – Provides social coaching/support.

No academic time will be compromised. In fact, academics may improve. Studies show that typical peers who engage in programs like FRIEND demonstrate improvements in academic achievement, problem-solving abilities, classroom and group participation, completion of homework, and improved empathy and self-esteem.

Your child was selected to participate in this program because they either volunteered or were recommended by school faculty. In order for your child to participate, we must have your permission.

Please complete the permission slip and return it to your child's teacher. We thank you for your consideration of this program and would be happy to answer any questions that you may have. For more information, please feel free to contact _____.

Sincerely,
(Name)
School Faculty

FRIEND® Permission Slip

Student's name: _____ Grade: _____

School: _____

Teacher: _____

Parent's name: _____

Address: _____

Phone: _____ Cell: _____

Work: _____

I give my permission for my child to participate in FRIEND (please circle):

Yes/No

Parent signature/date: _____

FRIEND® Contract

The contract below can be given to students in FRIEND® and other classmates too. It serves as a simple reminder of ways to be respectful and kind to all classmates, especially those who need support. Signing a contract is a way to emphasize the importance of this commitment and can also help them be accountable for supporting all their classmates.

FRIEND® Contract

I, _____, promise to be helpful and kind to all of my classmates before school, during school, at recess and lunch, and after school too. I will do my best to be respectful to all my classmates, even those who may look or act different than me. I recognize they have many things to offer, and they are not that different from me.

Some of the ways I can be helpful are:

1. Be aware when someone is alone and include them in what I am playing.

2. If they need help, I will show them or explain what to do.

3. If I am not sure what to do, I will ask a teacher for help.

4. If I see someone getting bullied or teased, I will ask the bullies to stop or help my classmate do something fun.

My two ideas to help my classmates are:

1. _____

2. _____

Student signature: _____ Date: _____

Teacher or parent signature: _____ Date: _____

Appendix II: FRIEND®
Planning Tools

It is important to document initial planning efforts of FRIEND® to identify roles and responsibilities. The Planning Tool can be completed at the first meeting. Agendas can help keep meetings focused and organized. Below are sample documents for planning and meetings to help keep FRIEND productive.

✓

FRIEND® Program Planning Tool

Student's name: _____   Date: _____

School: _____

FRIEND® Group Coordinator: _____

Next meeting date: _____

Team members:

Name	Position

FRIEND Roles and Responsibilities	Staff Assigned
Peer Sensitivity Training	
Baseline social skill assessments	
Playground Facilitator	
Selection of peer participants	
Orientation and ongoing training for: • Peer participants • Student with ASD	
Daily Lunch Group Facilitator	
FRIEND group meetings	
Ongoing data collection and evaluations	
School–parent working group	

Notes: _____

_____

_____

_____

FRIEND®: Initial Planning Meeting

Student: _____ Grade: _____

School: _____ Date: _____

Team members present: _____

I. FRIEND® program explanation

II. Roles and responsibilities

    a. FRIEND coordinator

    b. Daily support

    c. Parents

III. Peer Sensitivity Training

    a. Who/when/where

    b. Child—present/identified/diagnosis

    c. Other students with diagnosis

IV. FRIEND group members

    a. Suggestions

    b. Permission forms

V. FRIEND group meetings

    a. Location (speech office/classroom/cafeteria)

    b. How often (initially)

    c. Activities

    d. Assignments (food/materials)

VI. Follow-up meeting: _____

✓

FRIEND®: Follow-Up Meeting

Student: _____ Grade: _____

School: _____ Date: _____

Team members present: _____

I. Review from last meeting

II. Data

    a. Data on IEP goals since last meeting

    b. Number of FRIEND® group meetings/peer support meetings

III. Program successes

    a. Progress made

    b. Highlights of program

IV. Program challenges

    a. Significant challenges

    b. Problem solve/possible solutions

V. Support at home

    a. Prime student

    b. Skills to be taught/practiced at home

VI. Next meeting: _____

Appendix III: Social Functioning Interview

The Social Functioning Interview can help to collect qualitative information about the student's social functioning in different environments. It is a good way to document information that can be helpful when developing a FRIEND® program. On the following pages are two versions. One can be completed by an adult who knows the student well, and the other can be completed by the student. It is best to conduct both as an interview rather than a questionnaire to engage the respondent in a conversation about the student. This approach will help glean thoughtful and comprehensive information about the student's needs. These tools should be completed at the beginning of the program.

✓

Social Functioning Interview

Who is being interviewed: Parent/Teacher/Therapist (circle)

Name: _____

Address/School: _____

Phone number: _____

Student's name: _____

Grade: _____ Student's age: _____ Date completed: _____

Overview

   1. Strengths:

    _____

    _____

    _____

   2. Challenges:

    _____

    _____

    _____

Social functioning

   1. Please describe the student's social functioning including number of friends, frequency of socialization, and preferred social activities.

    _____

    _____

    _____

2. What does the student typically do at recess: Do they play alone or with other children? Do they join in games? Do they ask others to join them?

_____

_____

_____

3. Does the student seem anxious during social interactions? Do they avoid social situations?

_____

_____

_____

4. Does the student regulate their emotions according to the situation? Do they have temper tantrums or outbursts that typically end social interaction?

_____

_____

_____

5. Describe the student's nonverbal communication. Do they make, or maintain, eye contact during communication? Do they face students when speaking with them? Are their facial expressions varied, and do they communicate their feelings?

_____

_____

_____

Communication

1. Describe the student's language ability. Does the student ask questions? Are they conversational?

   _____

   _____

   _____

2. How would you describe the student's voice: too loud or too soft, monotone, odd pitch? Can adults and other children understand the student?

   _____

   _____

   _____

Interests

What are the student's interests? How often do they talk about or engage in these interests? Do they involve others in their interests?

_____

_____

_____

Behavior

Does the student have any odd or repetitive behaviors (hand-flapping, rocking, spinning, etc.)? Does the child have any sensory seeking, or sensory aversion behaviors that interfere with socialization?

_____

_____

_____

For the parent
Social opportunities at home

1. Does the student play with siblings or siblings' friends? Other family members?

    _____

    _____

    _____

2. Does the student play with any children in your community? How often? What kinds of activities do they play?

    _____

    _____

    _____

Social opportunities in the community

Describe any community activities your child participates in: scouts or other clubs, church or synagogue, sports, music, art, or theater groups.

_____

_____

_____

Recommendations for FRIEND® participants

1. _____

2. _____

3. _____

✓

Student Interview

Name: _____ Age: _____

Name of school: _____ Rater: _____

Classroom: _____ Date completed: _____

Interests and behaviors

1. What kind of things do you like to do?

   _____

   _____

   _____

2. Do any sounds or smells bother you? Does it bother you to be in a noisy, crowded room?

   _____

   _____

   _____

3. What do you want other students to know about you?

   _____

   _____

   _____

4. What do you have in common with other students?

   _____

   _____

   _____

Who would you like to be in this program with you?

   1. _____

   2. _____

   3. _____

Appendix IV: Super Skills Profile of Social Difficulty and Observation Recording Form

Collecting data at the beginning of FRIEND® can help to set appropriate goals for the student in the program. The tools in this appendix can help identify a student's specific social challenges and can also be repeated to help measure progress. The Super Skills Profile of Social Difficulty can be repeated two to three times within a school year. The Observation Recording Form targets specific observable behaviors during social interactions. This form can document successes of the program and identify areas that might require modification. Therefore, this form should be completed more frequently, even as often as once per week.

✓

Super Skills Profile of Social Difficulty

(Used with permission from Judith Coucouvanis: *Super Skills: A Social Skills Group Program for Children with Asperger Syndrome, High-Functioning Autism and Related Challenges*, 2005.)

Student's Name: _____ Age: _____ Date: _____

Recorder: _____

Relationship to Student: _____

Please mark the column you think applies to this student at present.

	Very Difficult	Difficult	Less Difficult	Neither Difficult Nor Easy	Less Easy	Easy	Very Easy
Fundamental Skills	0	1	2	3	4	5	6
Eye contact							
Correct Facial Expression							
Correct Voice Volume							
Correct Voice Tone							
Correct Timing							
Social Initiation Skills	0	1	2	3	4	5	6
Using Person's Name							
Using Farewells							
Greeting							
Introducing Self							
Asking for Help							
Giving a Compliment							
Starting a Conversation							
Joining a Conversation							

	0	1	2	3	4	5	6
Ending a Conversation							
Participating in a Conversation							
Inviting Someone To Play							
Introducing Others							
Joining In							
Talking About Self							
Making a Compliment							
Asking Appropriate Questions							
Offering an Opinion							
Expressing Basic Feelings							
Expressing Complex Feelings							
Social Response Skills	0	1	2	3	4	5	6
Responding to Greeting							
Responding to Compliments							
Listening							
Following Directions							
Making Short Comments							
Staying on the Topic							
Waiting							
Staying on Task							
Offering Help							
Giving Encouragement							
Reading Body Language							
Reading Feelings of Others							

✓

Dealing with Mistakes							
Dealing with Anger							
Refusing When Appropriate							
Getting Along With Others	0	1	2	3	4	5	6
Taking Turns							
Sharing							
Playing by the Rules							
Apologizing							
Being Fair							
Being a Good Sport							
Using Kind Talk							
Being Flexible							
Asking Permission							
Cooperating							
Dealing with "No"							
Compromising							
Dealing with a Problem							
Receiving a Suggestion							
Giving a Suggestion							
Letting Others Talk							
Showing Interest in Others							
Dealing with Teasing							

Observation Recording Form

Student's name:_____

Recorder's name:_____

School: _____

Duration of observation (please circle):

     5 minutes   10 minutes   other: _____

Operational definition

Social Initiations: A novel approach made by the target student toward a peer. If an interaction has not occurred for five seconds, and an approach occurs, then consider it a new initiation. An initiation can be either verbal or physical as long as it is socially appropriate. The initiation is counted even if the peer does not respond.

Duration of Engagement: Participating in an activity with a peer(s) such as playing a game, having a conversation, or simple cooperative play (drawing a picture with chalk on the playground). This does not include parallel play, or doing the same activity as peers without engagement, or watching a game that peers are playing. To add structure to the definition, timing of the engagement begins after five seconds of interaction and ends after five seconds of no interaction.

The five second rule allows the record-keeper adequate time to start the stop-watch. By adding five seconds to the end of the engagement the record-keeper won't short change the time engaged.

Social Initiation by Peer: A novel approach by a peer initiating an interaction with the target student. If an initiation by the peer has not occurred in five seconds, a new initiation may be counted. As before, the approach may be verbal or physical, but needs to be socially appropriate. An initiation is recorded even if the target student does not respond to the peer.

Social Responses: Any time a student responds to a peer within five seconds of the initiation by physically orienting to the peer and using socially appropriate nonverbal communicative gestures or verbally responding to the other student.

Negative Interaction: Any vocalization or gesture made by the peer or the target student that may offend or insult someone, for example, "You're stupid," or "He sucks at this game." Obviously, this kind of behavior should be minimized or eliminated in any program.

Behavior Key	+ Present
	0 Absent
	- Negative

Setting

Playground	Lunch

		Monday	Tuesday	Wednesday	Thursday	Friday	Total
Date							
Number of Social Initiations with Peers	Playground						
	Lunch						
Duration of Social Engagement	Playground						
	Lunch						
Number of Social Initiations from Peers	Playground						
	Lunch						

Number of Social Responses	Playground						
	Lunch						
Percent of Social Responses (social responses to peers divided by the total number of social initiations from peers)	Playground						
	Lunch						
Totals:							

General observations and comments: _____

_____

_____

_____

_____

_____

_____

_____

_____

_____

_____

_____

(e.g. sensory detractors, noise level, attitudes of peers toward student with ASD, activities of interest to student with ASD, social pragmatics)

Appendix V: Tip Sheets

Tips for Peers

Children with social challenges can learn things and have fun just like other kids. As you discover ways to enjoy spending time with a classmate with social challenges, you will learn that he or she is a neat kid. You will also feel better about yourself. Kids who learn to help other kids are often admired by their friends and teachers. You will also learn new things that are interesting and useful. Remember to always ask your teacher or school aide if you're not sure what to do, or how to be helpful and friendly to your classmate with social challenges.

- **Be respectful:** Treat others the way you would like to be treated. If a kid does something you don't like, instead of saying something mean, say something helpful. Offer a suggestion, "Hey, why don't you try it this way?"

- **Say "Hi":** Think about how you feel when your friends say "Hi," when you see them in the hall. When you pass someone in the hall, just say "Hi."

- **Offer your help:** If a child with differences needs help, don't be afraid to offer to help. If other kids are not being nice to another child, tell them to stop. If they don't stop, help the child being teased get away from a bad or hurtful situation.

- **Talk to them:** Talk to a child with differences like you would talk to another one of your friends. Don't be too formal and don't talk to them like they won't understand.

- **Be patient:** Sometimes it takes children with differences longer to do something or answer a question. Give them time to answer or do what they are asked.

- **Include:** Include children with differences in group activities like games and team sports. You can invite a child to sit next to you, hang out during recess or walk in the hall together. It's nice to be asked even if you're not interested. Don't feel badly if they say no.

- **Show:** Children with differences may have difficulty understanding rules, or knowing the right way to act or do things. Be helpful by showing them what to do. Don't just explain something to them; show them what to do. They can learn by watching you.

- **Support (but not too much):** Provide the right amount of help. Let your friends try to do things by themselves first, then help if they need it. That will make you feel good, and it will help them too.

- **Encourage:** Sometimes children with differences may be afraid to try new things. Praise them for trying, even if they don't get it right the first time. You can cheer, give "high-fives" or just tell them "Great work." They will be more willing to try again. Everyone needs a few tries to learn new things and everyone likes to be complimented.

- **Find something in common:** Some children with differences are great with math, spelling, or computers. They may have a great memory for the class schedule. Find something they like, such as a special skill or interest. You may find that your friends like lots of the same things. Try to find something in common, such as a favorite television show or game. A similarity can help you start a conversation, learn more about them, or even lead to new friendships.

- **It's okay:** It's okay to get frustrated with any child, including a child with differences. Don't feel bad if sometimes you want to play alone or with somebody else.

- **Ask:** There's a reason kids do things, even if it doesn't make sense to you. Try to figure it out so you can help them. If you're confused about something a child is doing, ask a teacher.

- **Learn:** Ask a teacher, your parents, or the parents of a child with differences about the child's challenges. Read on the internet or ask for some books. The more you learn about a child's challenges, the more you can be helpful and supportive.

Tips for Facilitators

Working together as a team will enable a child with social challenges to benefit from appropriate and consistent interventions throughout the day. As a parent you will be able to help them generalize skills with siblings, neighbors, and kids they meet in other community activities.

As an educational aide, playground or lunch supervisor, you can help a student successfully engage with their peers during less structured times. Remember, these are the most stressful and difficult times of the day for a child with social challenges. Here are some ideas to help you get started. Together, and throughout the school year, you'll be able to think of and implement other strategies uniquely helpful to students who need support.

- **Be present and supportive:** It is crucial that an adult is on the playground at recess, in the lunchroom, and is available during other unstructured times to facilitate social interactions. Social situations are challenging and some students avoid situations when they are unsure what to do.

- **Prepare for the activity:** It's possible to help the child with social challenges before recess by asking them what they want to do and setting up the activity with interested students. This kind of preparation can help both the child with social challenges and the facilitator plan for success.

- **Prompts:** Prompts are a helpful way to remind a child with social challenges what to do. For example, "Find someone to play with," encourages the child to use their own interests to decide whom to play with and what to do.

- **Peer models:** Identify children in the class who have similar interests, and encourage them to interact with the child with social challenges.

- **Encourage peers:** Encourage all kids to respond appropriately to the child with social challenges when the child approaches them. They can kindly support and reinforce appropriate behavior, which will increase motivation for the child to continue initiating interactions.

- **Provide additional support:** Once the child with social challenges begins to initiate a social interaction, the adult facilitator may need to provide some additional support or cues to ensure the interaction is a positive experience.

- **Special interests:** Special interests provide highly motivating opportunities for learning and social interactions. When staff members develop and implement games using a child's special interest, the desire to play with classmates increases. Not only does social behavior increase during that particular activity, but it increases at other times of the day as well.

- **Be patient:** Be aware that the child with social challenges may not show an interest in social activities initially. Like teaching academics or developing language, it will take time to motivate and support the child as they learn social skills and develop confidence.

Tips for Teachers

Students with social challenges are vulnerable at school and may be neglected or rejected by their classmates. Intervention and guidance from adult staff will help students with social challenges learn social and communication skills to develop healthy, satisfying friendships. We learn about the world from each other. Remember, teaching a child how to interact appropriately and comfortably with others provides them with the skills they'll need to be a valued classmate and successful employee, as well as a good friend.

In addition, all students in the general education classroom can benefit from an environment of acceptance and belonging. Social challenges and specific disorders (like ASD) are becoming more prevalent. As the prevalence of autism increases there will likely be more students with ASD in every classroom. If the typical students don't already have a neighbor or family member with ASD, most likely they eventually will. As typical peers interact with children with any social challenge they have daily opportunities to improve their own social and language skills, develop leadership, and demonstrate compassion and kindness.

- **Provide information:** Work with parents to provide peer sensitivity training to support ASD awareness. Provide peers a way to ask questions. For example, set up a question box in the classroom or identify an adult the students can go to for information. Teach typical students strategies for helping a classmate with social challenges during recess or lunchtime.

- **Create opportunities:** Create opportunities for students to practice social skills with games, class meetings, and cooperative learning experiences. Do your best to encourage friendships. Teach the importance of respecting each other.

- **Encourage responsiveness:** Encourage all students to respond appropriately to the individual with social challenges. They can kindly support and reinforce appropriate behavior.

- **Encourage mentors:** Encourage peers to become mentors or buddies to students with social challenges throughout the school day. A buddy can help a classmate with challenges line up before class, provide support during transitions, or even remind them to write their name on their paper.

- **Encourage independence:** Focus on ways the student with challenges can learn from others. For example, instead of saying, "Write your name on the paper," prompt the student by saying, "What are the other kids doing?" or "What comes next?"

- **Prepare:** Before going to recess or lunch, prepare the student with challenges. Ask them who they're going to play with and what they're going to do at recess.

- **Reinforce students:** Post a FRIENDSHIP poster in class; put a sticker on the poster each time a student engages in a friendly behavior toward another student. When the poster has a predetermined number of stickers, such as 25 or 50, reward the class with a special FRIENDSHIP game or treat.

- **Involve parents:** If a student is getting along well with a student with social challenges, let their parents know. They should be aware of the tolerance and compassion their child exhibits. You may even be able to encourage out-of-school activities.

✓

Tips for Parents

You can help your child learn to navigate the social world by teaching skills at home and providing opportunities to practice these skills in different places with different people. At first you may want to keep social interventions with other children short, structured, supervised, and voluntary. You are a facilitator, not a director, of the event. The best kind of supervision may be provided from a separate room when you can hear that everyone is having a good time. Your goal is to create successful experiences so that your child approaches new social opportunities with interest and confidence. Select activities that are motivating to both your child and their peers. With a little planning, everyone can have a good time with play dates, even you.

- **Learn:** Learn about age-appropriate social skills. Watch children your child's age. What are their interests? How do they play and communicate? Then encourage your child to be similar. Become familiar with current trends (fashion, toys, games/activities, music, television, films, and books) that are typical of your child's same-age peer group. Help your child become aware of and interested in these trends.

- **Teach conversation skills:** Teach your child to maintain conversations by responding appropriately or commenting on what someone has just said to them. Also, teach your child what not to say.

- **Teach social phrases:** Recognize age-appropriate phrases and encourage your child to use them. For example, if other kids are saying, "What's up?" or "I'm down with that," encourage your child to say it too.

- **Teach others:** Teach your child how to explain ASD and its characteristics to someone. Teach siblings, neighbors, and other family members how to socially interact with, and be a friend to, your child with challenges.

- **Practice at home:** Practice schoolyard games, sports, and activities at home so your child will be more familiar with them at school.

- **Role play:** Use role-play activities to practice cooperative play with another child. Make it structured and short.

- **Use family time:** Create social opportunities with family interactions such as reading a book together, playing board games, or watching movies together. Have each family member take turns picking a favorite book, game, or movie. This will help your child recognize the interests of other people and their benefits.

- **Laugh:** Help your child develop a sense of humor. Keep a joke book at the kitchen table, and take turns picking a favorite joke to read. It also might help to keep the family at the table longer.

- **Play:** Encourage your child to play appropriately with age-appropriate toys. For example, make the train go somewhere rather than lining it up. Play pretend games with your child. Incorporate their special interest to keep them motivated. For example, if they like weather, maybe there is a storm at the farm.

- **Create:** Create opportunities for your child to socially interact and communicate with their peers in natural settings. Set up social gatherings for your child with peers from school. Ask your child's teacher to suggest children to invite. Plan activities around particular themes, such as holidays or seasons, or highlight your child's interests, such as animals, presidents, music, Disney characters, or geography. Make these activities brief, structured, supervised, voluntary, and positive.

- **Communicate:** Communicate with your child's teachers, therapists, and other team members regarding what is happening at home. What was successful? What was motivating? What didn't work? This information can enrich your child's experience at school. Ask about what is happening at school with your child and about what the other kids are doing.

- **Get involved:** Become an active member of the school community by joining the parent–teacher organization and participating in the classroom or other school-wide events.

- **Groups:** Encourage your child to participate in programs that encourage cooperation and interaction. Join a choir, band, or

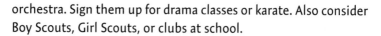

orchestra. Sign them up for drama classes or karate. Also consider Boy Scouts, Girl Scouts, or clubs at school.

- **Research:** Encourage your child to use the internet (supervised) to identify and develop friendships with others based on special interests, such as coin or stamp clubs, online games, chess clubs, and email friends.

Appendix VI: Implementation Checklists

Supervision is essential to an effective FRIEND® program. The supervisor can help the facilitator add structure to the program by providing feedback on the FRIEND activities. It can also be used to prompt the facilitator to consistently reinforce appropriate social behaviors.

✓

FRIEND® Lunch Checklist

Facilitator: _____ Supervisor: _____

Date: _____ Site: _____

Scoring

- Mark an X if the behavior occurs within the time interval.

- Mark an O if the behavior does not occur within the time interval.

- Mark N/A if the behavior is not applicable during that time interval.

General Instructions

Facilitator makes sure students are seated together at the lunch table and stays within close proximity of students.

Minute	5	10	15	20	25	30	Notes/Percentage
Encourages inclusion of the target student in appropriate conversations with peers							
Encourages peers to respond appropriately to all target student's social overtures							
Provides corrective guidance to inappropriate overtures							
Follows the lead of students when guiding/facilitating conversation topic							
Provides prompting to student with social challenges to participate in conversation							
Provides immediate reinforcement (within 5 seconds) for appropriate social behaviors for all students in the group							

Comments: _____

_____

_____

FRIEND® Playground Checklist

Facilitator: _____   Supervisor: _____

Date: _____   Site: _____

Scoring

- Mark an X if the behavior occurs within the time interval.

- Mark an O if the behavior does not occur within the time interval.

- Mark N/A if the behavior is not applicable during that time interval.

Minute	5	10	15	20	25	30	Notes/Percentage
Follows the lead of the target student when selecting activity (especially target students) *(If a child is interested in playing with the Frisbee, set up a cooperative activity that uses the Frisbee)*							
Sets up structured activity and prompts interactions (if target student does not provide lead) *(Sets up cooperative, turn-taking games)*							
Provides opportunities within activity for students to interact with one another *(Encourages working together while drawing with chalk or building something)*							
Prompts target student within activity as needed *(Encourages requesting a turn with peers)*							
Immediately (within 5 seconds of the behavior) reinforces appropriate social behaviors for both target and typical students *(Provides preferred item/praise, provides positive feedback)*							

cont.

Minute	5	10	15	20	25	30	Notes/Percentage
Prompts socially appropriate behavior and sets up opportunities to practice for both target and typical students							
(If the target student takes a toy from a peer without asking, sets up the opportunity again. Gives the toy back to the peer and tells the target student to ask the peer for the toy. When the child asks, provides praise, has the peer give the toy to the child for a turn. Provides praise to the peer. Encourages turn taking)							

Comments: _____

_____

_____

_____

_____

Fidelity of Implementation Checklist
for FRIEND® Lunch Program

Social Validity Form

Student's Name: _____

Evaluator's Name: _____

School Position: _____

School: _____ Date: _____

Circle the response that best describes how the FRIEND® Lunch Program intervention is going for the student with ASD and the peer participants.

SD=Strongly   D=Disagree   A=Agree   SA=Strongly Agree

I believe the FRIEND Lunch Program is beneficial to the student with ASD.

SD   D   A   SA

The peer participants are benefiting from this program.

SD   D   A   SA

The peer articipants have been adequately taught and know how to support the student with ASD.

SD   D   A   SA

The student with ASD has adequate support during the FRIEND Lunch Program to learn skills and feel successful.

SD   D   A   SA

The peer participants have adequate support during the FRIEND Lunch Program to learn skills and feel successful.

SD   D   A   SA

The student with ASD is enjoying the FRIEND Lunch Program.

SD   D   A   SA

The peer participants are enjoying the FRIEND® Lunch Program.

     SD   D   A   SA

The FRIEND Lunch Program is easy to implement.

     SD   D   A   SA

I enjoy being part of this intervention.

     SD   D   A   SA

I intend to implement the FRIEND Lunch Program for other students with social differences.

     SD   D   A   SA

Comments: _____

_____

_____

_____

_____

_____

_____

_____

_____

_____

_____

_____

_____

_____

_____

_____

Fidelity of Implementation Checklist for FRIEND® Playground Program

Social Validity Form

Student's Name: _____

Evaluator's Name: _____

School Position: _____

School: _____ Date: _____

Circle the response that best describes how the FRIEND® Playground Program intervention is going for the student with ASD and their classmates on the playground.

SD=Strongly   D=Disagree   A=Agree   SA=Strongly Agree

I believe the FRIEND Playground Program is beneficial to the student with ASD.

SD   D   A   SA

The other students on the playground are benefiting from this program.

SD   D   A   SA

Students on the playground have been adequately taught and know how to support the student with ASD.

SD   D   A   SA

The student with ASD has adequate support during the FRIEND Playground Program to learn skills and feel successful.

SD   D   A   SA

The other students on the playground have adequate support during the FRIEND Playground Program to learn skills and feel successful.

SD   D   A   SA

The student with ASD is enjoying the FRIEND Playground Program.

SD   D   A   SA

Students on the playground are enjoying the FRIEND® Playground Program.

     SD   D   A   SA

The FRIEND Playground Program is easy to implement.

     SD   D   A   SA

I enjoy being part of this intervention.

     SD   D   A   SA

I intend to implement the FRIEND Playground Program for other students with social differences.

     SD   D   A   SA

Comments: _____

_____

_____

_____

_____

_____

_____

_____

_____

_____

_____

_____

_____

_____

_____

_____

Appendix VII: FRIEND®
Activity Guide

Land of Shapes

Grades: 2–5

Estimated time: 25–30 minutes

OBJECTIVES

- Students will discover the usefulness of combining things that are different to make other beautiful objects.

- Students will recognize and appreciate the differences around them.

MATERIALS/PREPARATION

- Pictures of shapes to share with students while reading the story (provided)

- Different color shapes for pairs of students to explore and create with after the story

- Scissors to cut out shapes (optional)

- Heavy paper or cardstock to mount the new pictures for each pair of students

- Glue or tape to mount the shapes on the heavy paper (have several pairs of students share one or two)

PROCEDURE

Tell the following story:

"Today we are going to take a trip to the Land of Shapes. In this land lived all kinds of shapes. What do you notice about the way the shapes lived in the land?" *(They are grouped together according to which kind of shape they are.)*

"You see, in the land of shapes, there was a rule. No one ever talked about the rule, but everyone knew about it. The rule was that shapes of different kinds could not get mixed up with each other. You had to stay 'with your own kind' in the land of shapes. All the shapes stayed in their own part of the land. Everybody knew the rule and everybody obeyed it.

Then one day, something strange happened. This big pink circle was playing around and he stumbled and fell. As he fell, he started to roll. He tried as hard as he could to stop himself, but as hard as he tried, he could not stop. He was rolling, faster and faster, to the land of triangles. And finally, he rolled smack into a brown triangle. The pink circle was surprised at what he had done, and the brown triangle was surprised at what had happened to him.

But as they looked at what had happened to them, they discovered the most surprising thing. They had turned into an ice cream cone; the first ice cream cone there had ever been in the land of shapes; and a delicious ice cream cone they were too.

Now, all the other shapes in the land had been watching what was happening to the circle and the triangle. They had seen what a wonderful thing had happened because the pink circle had ended up in the land of triangles. The shapes began to wonder about this rule. They began to think that perhaps it wasn't such a good rule after all. They decided that they would break the rule.

The shapes began to think about what would happen if they got all mixed up with each other. They began to think of all the things they could become. They thought and thought about what they could make if they all got together. Finally, they decided on what they wanted to become." *(Without telling the children what the shapes have decided to make, begin putting the shapes together. Let the children discover that the shapes are turning into a butterfly.)*

"The shapes made sure that they found a place for each and every shape in the land.

Now that they had turned themselves into a butterfly, they discovered that they were beautiful, and they discovered that they could visit all the flowers in the garden. They could do so many wonderful things that they never could do when they had stayed with their own kind."

Discussion questions

What can we learn from the story of the Land of Shapes?

1. All things are different and that's okay.

2. It takes lots of things that are different to make something useful, beautiful, or special.

3. If things that are different are kept apart, they can't work together to make special things happen.

Here are two important lessons for us to remember:

1. Different is okay.

2. When we put different things together, something special happens.

ACTIVITIES

- Have the students pair up with another student they do not know very well.

- Give each pair a set of different colored shapes (for best experience, give each group different sets of shapes and colors).

- Instruct each pair to create a common object or shape (such as the ice cream cone) with their shapes.

- For variation: two to four pairs can sit at a table together so they can trade shapes or colors if desired. They can share glue/tape and scissors, which will encourage a greater cooperative learning experience.

ACADEMIC STANDARDS

- *Language Arts* – Uses listening and speaking strategies for different purposes.

- *Language Arts* – Uses reading skills and strategies to understand and interpret a variety of informational texts.

- *Thinking and Reasoning* – Effectively uses mental processes that are based on identifying similarities and differences.

- *Mathematics* – Understands and applies basic and advanced properties of the concepts of geometry.

- *Behavioral Studies* – Understands that group and cultural influences contribute to human development, identity, and behavior.

Positive Reinforcement Chart

Grades: 2–5

OBJECTIVES

- Students will demonstrate kindness, and supportive and helpful behaviors toward one another.

MATERIALS/PREPARATION

- A large piece of black or white poster board
- Colorful stickers in a variety of geometric shapes
- A drawn outline of a butterfly on the white poster board or a cut-out shape of a butterfly from the black poster board mounted on a contrasting background

PROCEDURES

- When a student demonstrates an act of kindness or support, is helpful, or says something nice to another individual, provide positive reinforcement by adding a sticker to the butterfly chart.
- The motivation to acquire stickers and fill in the butterfly wings to become a beautiful mosaic of colorful shapes will support a classroom community of caring and respectful individuals.

ACADEMIC STANDARDS

- *Behavioral Studies* – Understands various meanings of social group, general implications of group membership, and different ways that groups function.
- *Behavioral Studies* – Understands that interactions among learning, inheritance, and physical development affect human behavior.
- *Visual Arts* – Understands the characteristics and merits of one's own artwork and the artwork of others.

Spread Your Wings

Grades: 2–5

Estimated time : 15–20 minutes

OBJECTIVES

- Students will imagine different places to explore.
- Students will work with a small group to collectively make a decision.
- Students will discover the benefits of helping one another.

MATERIALS/PREPARATION

- Paper for each group
- Pen/pencils for each group
- Optional: crayons/markers for each group to draw a picture

PROCEDURES

- Divide the students into small groups of three or four, preferably randomized (i.e. have the students count to a number and all the 1's are a group, 2's are a group, etc.).
- Ask the students, "If you had wings, where would you go?" Let them talk about it within their groups and learn about the different places each one would go within the group. Then have each group decide on one destination and write it down. Make sure each group understands that every member of the group needs to go to this place together.
- Now tell one student in each group they don't have wings but everyone else in the group does. Have the students discuss in their groups how they can help their friend without wings get to the place they chose.

FOLLOW UP

- The groups can demonstrate through role play and discuss how they will travel to their destinations together.

- Have the groups draw pictures of their chosen places and how they have decided to go there and share with the rest of the class.

- Have each student write a short story describing their "ideal" place they would travel to with wings and their efforts helping someone who doesn't have wings.

ACADEMIC STANDARDS

- *Behavioral Studies* – Understands conflict, cooperation, and interdependence among individuals, groups, and institutions.

- *Thinking and Reasoning* – Understands and applies the basic principles of presenting an argument.

- *Working with Others* – Works well with diverse individuals and in diverse situations.

- *Language Arts* – Uses listening and speaking strategies for different purposes.

Fast/Slow

Grades: 2–5

Estimated time: 20–30 minutes

OBJECTIVES

- Students will dance to the provided music as directed.

- Students will discover how music and other people can influence their movements or actions.

- Students will explore their individuality among a group of their peers.

MATERIALS/PREPARATION

- Equipment to play recorded music (CD player/boom box/mp3 player)

- Two chosen pieces of recorded music

- Optional: if recorded music is unavailable, use drums, shakers, or sticks to provide a steady beat or pulse

PROCEDURE

- Select two pieces of music: one to help your students move fast (e.g. "Flight of the Bumblebee" or popular song your kids may know) and another to help your students move slowly (e.g. "Blue Danube Waltz" or other popular song your kids may know).

- Divide your class in half and instruct one half of the students to move fast around the room and the other half to move slowly around the room (to help the students, they could be instructed to fly like butterflies, or move like other animals specific to fast or slow) while the music is playing. Be sure that they understand that they must move as directed regardless of what the music or their peers make them feel like doing.

- Play either piece of music for a short time (30 seconds to 1 minute), then stop it. Have the students stop when the music stops.

- Now play the other piece of music (for the same duration) and do the same activity, with the kids moving the same as before.

- Variation: Instead of grouping the students in half, arrange them into small groups of four or five. Instruct them to stay together as a group as they are dancing (they could clap their hands, jump, stomp their feet, or use other movement in place to avoid confusion). Designate one member of the group to move in the opposite way to the others in the group. Play the music as above.

FOLLOW UP
Discussion questions

1. How did it feel to have other kids moving differently than you?

2. How did it feel to try to move fast/slow, when the music was moving differently than you?

3. Did you try to ask your friends to move fast/slow with you? How would you feel if they couldn't?

4. What could you do to move with your friends even though they may not be able to move as fast/slow as you?

ACADEMIC STANDARDS

- *Dance* – Identifies and demonstrates movement elements and skills in performing dance.

- *Music* – Knows and applies appropriate criteria to music and music performances.

- *Behavioral Studies* – Understands that group and cultural influences contribute to human development, identity, and behavior.

- *Thinking and Reasoning* – Effectively uses mental processes that are based on identifying similarities and differences.

- *Physical Education* – Uses a variety of basic and advanced movement forms.

Bibliography

American Academy of Pediatrics (2006) Understanding autism spectrum disorders (ASDs)(Handout).

American Academy of Pediatrics (2013) The crucial role of recess in school (Policy Statement).

Asher, S.R., Parker, J.G., and Walker, D.L. (1998) 'Distinguishing Friendship from Acceptance: Implications for Intervention and Assessment.' In W.M. Bukowski, A.F. Newcomb, and W.W. Hartup (eds) *The Company They Keep: Friendship in Childhood and Adolescence.* New York: Cambridge University Press.

Attwood, T. (1998) *Asperger's Syndrome: A Guide for Parents and Professionals.* London: Jessica Kingsley Publishers.

Attwood, T. (2007) *The Complete Guide to Asperger's Syndrome.* London: Jessica Kingsley Publishers.

Baker, B.L., Koegel, R.L., and Koegel, L.K. (1998) 'Increasing the social behavior of young children with autism using their obsessive behaviors.' *Journal of The Association for Persons with Severe Handicaps 23,* 300–308.

Baker, J.E. (2003) *Social Skills Training for Students with Asperger's Syndrome and Related Social Communication Disorders.* Shawnee Mission, KS: Autism Asperger Publishing Company.

Baker, M.J. (2000) 'Incorporating the thematic ritualistic behaviors of children with autism into games: Increasing social play interactions with siblings.' *Journal of Positive Behavior Interventions 2,* 2, 66–84.

Barrett, W. and Randall, L. (2004) 'Investigating the circle of friends approach: Adaptations and implications for practice.' *Educational Psychology in Practice 20,* 4, 353–368.

Bass, J.D. and Mulick, J.A. (2007) 'Social play skill enhancement of children with autism using peers and siblings as therapists.' *Psychology in the Schools 44,* 7, 727–735.

Bauminger, N. and Kasari, C. (2000) 'Loneliness and friendship in high-functioning children with autism.' *Child Development 71,* 447–456.

Bauminger, N. and Shulman, C. (2003) 'The development and maintenance of friendship in high-functioning children with autism: Maternal perceptions.' *SAGE Publications and The National Autistic Society 7,* 1, 81–97.

Bauminger, N., Shulman, C., and Agam, G. (2003) 'Peer interaction and loneliness in high-functioning children with autism.' *Journal of Autism and Developmental Disorders 33*, 5, 489–507.

Bauminger, N., Solomon, M., Aviezer, A., Heung, K., Brown, J., and Rogers, S.J. (2008) 'Friendship in high-functioning children with autism spectrum disorder: Mixed and non-mixed dyads.' *Journal of Autism and Developmental Disorders 38*, 1211–1229.

Bellini, S. (2004) 'Social skill deficits and anxiety in high-functioning adolescents with autism spectrum disorders.' *Focus on Autism and Other Developmental Disabilities 19*, 2, 78–86.

Bellini, S. (2006a) *Building Social Relationships: A Systematic Approach to Teaching Social Interaction Skills to Children and Adolescents with Autism Spectrum Disorders and Other Social Difficulties.* Shawnee Mission, KS: Autism Asperger Publishing Company.

Bellini, S. (2006b) 'The development of social anxiety in adolescents with autism spectrum disorders.' *Focus on Autism and Other Developmental Disabilities 21*, 3, 138–145.

Bellini, S., Peters, J.K., Benner, L., and Hopf, A. (2007) 'A meta-analysis of school-based social skills interventions for children with autism spectrum disorders.' *Remedial and Special Education 28*, 3, 153–162.

Boutot, E.A. and Bryant, D.P. (2005) 'Social integration of students with autism in inclusive settings.' *Education and Training in Developmental Disabilities 40*, 1, 14–23.

Bowers, L., Huisingh, R., and LoGiudice, C. (2007) *Tasks of Problem Solving: Adolescent.* East Moline, IL: LinguiSystems, Inc.

Boyd, B.A., Conroy, M.A., Mancil, G.R., Nakao, T., and Alter, P.J. (2007) 'Effects of circumscribed interests on the social behaviors of children with autism spectrum disorders.' *Journal of Autism and Developmental Disorders 37*, 1550–1561.

Bracken, B.A. (1992) *Examiner's Manual for the Multidimensional Self-esteem Scale.* Austin, TX: Pro-Ed, Inc.

Bunch, G. (2004) 'Typical student attitudes toward peers with disabilities in inclusive and special education schools.' *British Journal of Disability and Society 19*, 1, 61–76.

Callahan, K., Henson, R.K., and Cowan, A.K. (2008) 'Social validation of evidence-based practices in autism by parents, teachers, and administrators.' *Journal of Autism and Developmental Disabilities 38*, 678–692.

Carrow-Woolfolk, E. (1999) *Comprehensive Assessment of Spoken Language (CASL).* Circle Pines, MN: American Guidance Service.

Carter, E.W., Cushing, L.S., and Kennedy, C.H. (2009) *Peer Support Strategies for Improving All Students' Social Lives and Learning.* Baltimore, MD: Paul H. Brookes Publishing Company, Inc.

Carter, E.W., Hughes, C., Copeland, S.R., and Breen, C. (2001) 'Differences between high school students who do and do not volunteer to participate in peer interaction programs.' *Journal of the Association for Persons with Severe Handicaps 26*, 229–239.

Carter, E.W. and Kennedy, C.H. (2006) 'Promoting access to the general curriculum using peer support strategies.' *Research & Practice for Persons with Severe Disabilities 31*, 4, 284–292.

Centers for Disease Control and Prevention (CDC) (2014) Autism Spectrum Disorder. Retrieved from www.cdc.gov/ncbddd/autism

Chamberlain, B., Kasari, C., and Rotheram-Fuller, E. (2007) 'Involvement or isolation? The social networks of children with autism in regular classrooms.' *Journal of Autism and Developmental Disorders 37*, 230–242.

Chiang, H. and Carter, M. (2008) 'Spontaneity of communication in individuals with autism.' *Journal of Autism and Developmental Disorders 38*, 693–705.

Chin, H.Y. and Bernard-Opitz, V. (2000) 'Teaching conversational skills to children with autism: Effect on the development of a theory of mind.' *Journal of Autism and Developmental Disorders 30*, 6, 569–583.

Cleave, J.V. and Davis, M.M. (2006) 'Bullying and peer victimization among children with special health care needs.' *Pediatrics 118*, e1212–e1219.

Colvin, G., Sugai, G., Good, R. H. III, and Lee, Y.-Y. (1997) 'Using active supervision and pre-correction to improve transition behaviors in an elementary school.' *School Psychology Quarterly 12*, 4, 344–363.

Constantino, J. and Gruber, J. (2005) *Social Responsiveness Scale (SRS) Manual.* Los Angeles, CA: Western Psychological Services.

Copeland, S.R., Hughes, C., Carter, E.W., Guth, C., Presley, J., and Williams, C.R. (2004) 'Increasing access to general education: Perspectives of participants in a high school peer support program.' *Remedial and Special Education 26*, 342–352.

Corbett, B.A., Schupp, C.W., Simon, D., Ryan, N., and Mendoza, S. (2010) 'Elevated cortisol during play is associated with age and social engagement in children with autism.' *Molecular Autism 1*, 13, 1–12.

Coucouvanis, J. (2005) *Super Skills: A Social Skills Group Program for Children with Asperger Syndrome, High-Functioning Autism and Related Challenges.* Shawnee Mission, KS: Autism Asperger Publishing Company.

Cowan, R.J. and Allen, K.D. (2007) 'Using naturalistic procedures to enhance learning in individuals with autism: A focus on generalized teaching within the school setting.' *Psychology in the Schools 44*, 7, 701–715.

Cowie, H. and Wallace, P. (2000) *Peer Support in Action: From Bystanding to Standing By.* London: Sage Publications.

Cushing, L.S. and Kennedy, C.H. (1997) 'Academic effects of providing peer support in general education classrooms on students without disabilities.' *Journal of Applied Behavior Analysis 30,* 139–152.

Dawson, G. and Adams, A. (1984) 'Imitation and social responsiveness in autistic children.' *Journal of Abnormal Psychology 12*, 209–225.

Dodge, K.A., Schlundt, D.C., Schocken, I., and Delugach, J.D. (1983) 'Social competence and children's sociometric status: The role of peer group entry strategies.' *Merrill-Palmer Quarterly 29*, 309–336.

Doody, K. and Mertz, J. (2013) 'Preferred play activities of children with autism spectrum disorder in naturalistic settings.' *North American Journal of Medicine and Science 6*, 3, 128–133.

Doran, G.T. (1981) 'There's a S.M.A.R.T. way to write management's goals and objectives.' *Management Review 70*, 11, 35–36.

Eckerman, C.O. and Stein, M.R. (1982) 'The Toddler's Emerging Interactive Skills.' In K.H. Rubin and H.S. Ross (eds) *Peer Relationships and Social Skills in Childhood.* New York: Springer-Verlag.

Education for All Handicapped Children Act (1975) Washington, DC: US Government Printing Office.

Faherty, C. (2000) *Asperger's... What Does It Mean to Me? A Workbook Explaining Self Awareness and Life Lessons to the Child or Youth with High Functioning Autism or Asperger's.* Arlington, TX: Future Horizons, Inc.

Fisher, D. (1999) 'According to their peers: Inclusion as high school students see it.' *Mental Retardation 37*, 6, 458–467.

Fisher, M. and Meyer, L.H. (2002) 'Development and social competence after two years for students enrolled in inclusive and self-contained educational programs.' *Research & Practice for Persons with Severe Disabilities 27*, 3, 165–174.

Fitzgerald, M. (2007) 'Suicide and Asperger's syndrome.' *Crisis 28*, 1, 1–3.

Forest, M. and Pearpoint, J. (1991) 'Common sense tools: MAPS and CIRCLES for inclusive education.' *Journal of the National Center for Outcome Based Education 1*, 3, 27–37.

Frederickson, N., Warren, L., and Turner, J. (2005) '"Circle of friends" – an exploration of impact over time.' *Educational Psychology in Practice 21*, 3, 197–217.

Garvey, C. (1977) *Play.* Cambridge, MA: Harvard University Press.

Gena, A. (2006) 'The effects of prompting and social reinforcement on establishing social interactions with peers during the inclusion of four children with autism in preschool.' *International Journal of Psychology 41*, 6, 541–554.

Gibson, E.J. and Pick, A.D. (2000) *An Ecological Approach to Perceptional Learning and Development.* Oxford: Oxford University Press.

Goldstein, H., Schneider, N., and Thiemann, K. (2007) 'Peer-mediated social communication intervention: When clinical expertise informs treatment development and evaluation.' *Topics in Language Disorders 27*, 2, 182–199.

Greenway, C. (2000) 'Autism and asperger syndrome: Strategies to promote prosocial behaviours.' *Educational Psychology in Practice 16*, 3, 469–486.

Gresham, F.M. (1984) 'Social skills and self-efficacy for exceptional children.' *Exceptional Children 51*, 253–361.

Gresham, F.M. and Elliott, S.N. (2008) *Social Skills Improvement System: Rating Scales.* Bloomington, MN: Pearson Assessments.

Gresham, F.M. and Lambros, K.M. (1998) 'Behavioral and Functional Assessment.' In T.S. Watson and F.M. Gresham (eds) *Issues in Clinical Child Psychology: Handbook of Child Behavior Therapy.* New York: Plenum Press.

Gresham, F.M., Sugai, G., and Horner, R.H. (2001) 'Interpreting outcomes of social skills training for students with high-incidence disabilities.' *Exceptional Children 67*, 3, 331–334.

Gus, L. (2000) 'Autism: Promoting peer understanding.' *Educational Psychology in Practice 16*, 3, 461–468.

Hall, L.J. and Smith, K.L. (1996) 'The generalization of social skills by preferred peers with autism.' *Journal of Intellectual & Developmental Disability 21*, 4, 313–331.

Harper, G.F. and Maheady, L. (2007) 'Peer-mediated teaching and students with learning disabilities.' *Intervention in School and Clinic 43*, 2, 101–107.

Harper, C.B., Symon, J.B.G., and Frea, W.D. (2008) 'Recess is time-in: Using peers to improve social skills of children with autism.' *Journal of Autism and Developmental Disorders 38*, 815–826.

Harrison, P.L. and Oakland, T. (2003) *Adaptive Behavior Assessment —Second Edition Manual (ABASII).* San Antonio, TX: Harcourt Assessment.

Harrower, J.K. and Dunlap, G. (2001) 'Including children with autism in general education classrooms: A review of effective strategies.' *Behavior Modification 25*, 5, 762–784.

Hartup, W.W. (1983) 'Peer Relations.' In E.M. Hetherington (ed.) *Handbook of Child Psychology: Volume 4. Socialization, Personality, and Social Development.* New York: Wiley.

Hauck, M., Fein, D., Waterhouse, L., and Feinstein, C. (1995) 'Social initiations by autistic children to adults and other children.' *Journal of Autism and Developmental Disorders 25*, 579–595.

Hay, D., Payne, A., and Chadwick, A. (2004) 'Peer relations in childhood.' *Journal of Child Psychology and Psychiatry 45*, 84–108.

Hoff, K.E. and DuPaul, G.J. (1998) 'Reducing disruptive behavior in general education classrooms: The use of self-management strategies.' *School Psychology Review 27*, 290–303.

Horrocks, J.L., White, G., and Roberts, L. (2008) 'Principals' attitudes regarding inclusion of children with autism in Pennsylvania public schools.' *Journal of Autism and Developmental Disorders 38*, 1462–1473.

Howlin, P., Mawhood, L., and Rutter, M.J. (2000) 'Autism and developmental receptive language disorder—a follow-up comparison in early adult life. II: Social, behavioural, and psychiatric outcomes.' *Journal of Child Psychology and Psychiatry 41*, 5, 561–578.

Hughes, C., Copeland, S.R., Guth, C., Rung, L.L., *et al.* (2001) 'General education students' perspective on their involvement in a high school peer buddy program.' *Education and Training in Mental Retardation and Developmental Disabilities 36*, 343–356.

Huisingh, R., Bowers, L., and LoGiudice. C. (2006) *The Listening Comprehension Test—2.* East Moline, IL: LinguiSystems, Inc.

Hume, K., Bellini, S., and Pratt, C. (2005) 'The usage and perceived outcomes of early childhood programs for young children with autism spectrum disorder.' *Topics in Early Childhood Special Education 25*, 4, 195–207.

Hurth, J., Shaw, E., Izeman, S., Whaley, K., and Rogers, S. (1999) 'Areas of agreement about effective practices serving young children with autism spectrum disorders.' *Infants and Young Children 12*, 17–26.

Hyten, C. and Burns, R. (1986) 'Social Relations and Social Behavior.' In H.W. Reese and L.J. Parrott (eds) *Behavior Science: Philosophical, Methodological, and Empirical Advances.* Hillsdale, NJ: Lawrence Erlbaum Associates.

Individuals with Disabilities Education Act (1997) Washington, DC: US Government Printing Office.

Individuals with Disabilities Education Act (2004) Washington, DC: US Government Printing Office.

Ingersoll, B. and Schreibman, L. (2006) 'Teaching reciprocal imitation skills to young children with autism using a naturalistic behavioral approach: Effects on language, pretend play, and joint attention.' *Journal of Autism and Developmental Disorders 36*, 4, 487–505.

Jackson, L. and Panyan, M. (2002) *Positive Behavioral Support in the Classroom.* Baltimore, MD: Paul H. Brookes Publishing Co.

Johnson, D.W. and Johnson, R.T. (1984) 'Classroom Structure and Attitudes Toward Handicapped Students in Mainstream Settings: A Theoretical Model and Research Evidence.' In R.L. Jones (ed.) *Attitudes and Attitude Change in Special Education: Theory and Practice.* Reston, VA: Council for Exceptional Children.

Kaiser, A.P., Hancock, T.B., and Nietfeld, J.P. (2000) 'The effects of parent-implemented enhanced milieu teaching on the social communication of children who have autism.' *Journal of Early Education and Development 4,* 423–446.

Kalyva, E. and Avramidis, E. (2005) 'Improving communication between children with autism and their peers through the "circle of friends": A small-scale intervention study.' *Journal of Applied Research in Intellectual Disabilities 18,* 253–261.

Kamps, D.M., Kravits, T., Lopez, A.G., Kemmerer, K., Potucek, J., and Harrell, L.G. (1998) 'What do the peers think? Social validity of peer-mediated programs.' *Education and Treatment of Children 21,* 2, 107–135.

Kamps, D.M., Leonard, B.R., Vernon, S., Dugan, E.P., and Delquadri, J.C. (1992) 'Teaching social skills to students with autism to increase peer interactions in an integrated first-grade classroom.' *Journal of Applied Behavior Analysis 25,* 2, 281–288.

Kamps, D., Royer, J., Dugan, E., Kravits, T., *et al.* (2002) 'Peer training to facilitate social interaction for elementary students with autism and their peers.' *Exceptional Children 68,* 2, 173–187.

Kasari, C., Locke, J., Gulsrud, A., Rotheram-Fuller, C. (2010). 'Social networks and friendships at school: Comparing children with and without ASD.' *Journal of Autism and Developmental Disorders,* DOI 10.1007/s10803-01001076-x.

Kasari, C., Roheram-Fuller, E., Locke, J., and Gulsrud, A. (2012) 'Making the connection: Randomized controlled trial of social skills at school for children with autism spectrum disorders.' *Journal of Child Psychology and Psychiatry 53,* 4, 431–439.

Kashinath, S., Woods, J., and Goldstein, H. (2008) 'Enhancing generalized teaching strategy use in daily routines by parents of children with autism.' *Journal of Speech, Language, and Hearing Research 49,* 466–485.

Kennedy, C.H. and Itkonen, T. (1996) 'Social Relationships, Influential Variables, and Change across the Life Span.' In L.K. Koegel, R.L. Koegel, and G. Dunlap (eds) *Positive Behavioral Support: Including People with Difficult Behavior in the Community.* Baltimore, MD: Paul H. Brookes Publishing Co.

Kern, L., Vorndran, C.M., Hilt, A., Ringdahl, J.E., Adelman, B.E., and Dunlap, G. (1998) 'Choice as an intervention to improve behavior: A review of the literature.' *Journal of Behavioral Education 8,* 151–169.

Kernan, M. (2005) 'Developing citizenship through supervised play: The Civics Institute of Ireland playgrounds, 1933–75.' *History of Education 34,* 6, 675–687.

Kishi, G.S. and Meyer, L.H. (1994) 'What children report and remember: A six-year follow-up of the effects of social contact between peers with and without severe disabilities.' *Journal of the Association for Persons with Severe Handicaps 19,* 277–289.

Klein, G.W. and Reynolds, P.H. (2008) *Wings of EPOH.* Dedham, MA: FableVision, Inc.

Knapczyk, D. and Rodes, P. (2001) *Teaching Social Competence: Social Skills and Academic Success.* Verona, WI: IEP Resources.

Koegel, L.K., Carter, C.M., and Koegel, R.L. (2003) 'Teaching children with autism self-initiations as a pivotal response.' *Topics in Language Disorders 23,* 2, 134–145.

Koegel, L.K., Koegel, R.L., Hurley, C., and Frea, W.D. (1992) 'Improving social skills and disruptive behavior in children with autism through self-management.' *Journal of Applied Behavioral Analysis 25*, 2, 341–353.

Koegel, L.K. and LaZebnik, C. (2004) *Overcoming Autism: Finding the Answers, Strategies, and Hope That Can Transform a Child's Life.* New York: Penguin.

Koegel, R., Bimbela, A., and Schreibman, L. (1996) 'Collateral effects of parent training on family interactions.' *Journal of Autism and Developmental Disorders 30*, 383–391.

Koegel, R.L., Dyer, K., and Bell, L.K. (1987) 'The influence of child-preferred activities on autistic children's social behavior.' *Journal of Applied Behavior Analysis 20*, 243–252.

Koegel, R.L., Koegel, L.K., and Carter, C.M. (1999) 'Pivotal teaching interactions for children with autism.' *School Psychology Review 28*, 4, 576–594.

Koegel, R.L., Werner, G.A., Vismara, L.A., and Koegel, L.K. (2005) 'The effectiveness of contextually supported play date interactions between children with autism and typically developing peers.' *Research and Practice for Persons with Severe Disabilities 30*, 2, 93–102.

Kohler, F.W., Greteman, C., Raschke, D., and Highnam, C. (2007) 'Using a buddy skills package to increase the social interactions between a preschooler with autism and her peers.' *Topics in Early Childhood Special Education 27*, 3, 155–163.

Kohler, F.W., Strain, P.S., Hoyson, M., and Jamieson, B. (1997) 'Merging naturalistic teaching and peer-based strategies to address the IEP objectives of preschoolers with autism: An examination of structural and child behavior outcomes.' *Focus on Autism and Other Developmental Disabilities 12*, 4, 196–206.

Krajewski, J.J., Hyde, M.S., and O'Keefe, M.K. (2002) 'Teen attitudes toward individuals with mental retardation from 1987–1998: Has inclusion made a difference?' *Education and Training in Mental Retardation and Developmental Disabilities 35*, 284–293.

La Greca, A.M. (1999) 'The social anxiety scales for children and adolescents.' *The Behavior Therapist 22*, 7, 133–136.

Laugeson, E.A., Frankel, F., Gantman, A., Dillon, A.R., and Mogil, C. (2012) 'Evidence-based social skills training for adolescents with autism spectrum disorders: The UCLA PEERS program.' *Journal of Autism and Developmental Disorders 42*, 6, 1025–1036.

Laushey, K.M. and Heflin, L.J. (2000) 'Enhancing social skills of kindergarten children with autism through the training of multiple peers as tutors.' *Journal of Autism and Developmental Disorders 30*, 3, 183–193.

Lee, S., Odom, S.L., and Loftin, R. (2007) 'Social engagement with peers and stereotypic behavior of children with autism.' *Journal of Positive Behavior Interventions 9*, 2, 67–79.

Lemanek, K.L., Stone, W.L., and Fischel, P.T. (1993) 'Parent–child interactions in handicapped preschoolers: The relation between parent behaviors and compliance.' *Journal of Applied Behavior Analysis 21*, 4, 391–400.

Lindon, J. (2001) *Understanding Children's Play.* Cheltenham: Nelson Thornes.

Lindsay, G. (2007) 'Educational psychology and the effectiveness of inclusive education/ mainstreaming.' *British Journal of Educational Psychology 77*, 1–24.

Little, L. (2002) 'Middle-class mothers' perceptions of peer and sibling victimization among children with Asperger's syndrome and nonverbal learning disorders.' *Issues in Comprehensive Pediatric Nursing 25*, 43–57.

Lleras, C. (2008) 'Do skills and behaviors in high school matter? The contribution of noncognitive factors in explaining differences in educational attainment and earnings.' *Social Science Research 37*, 3, 888–902.

Locke, J., Ishijima, E.H., Kasari, C., and London, N. (2010) 'Loneliness, friendship quality and the social networks of adolescents with high-functioning autism in an inclusive school setting.' *Journal of Research in Special Education Needs 10*, 2, 74–81.

MacDonald, M., Lord, C., and Ulrich, D. (2013) 'The relationship of motor skills and social communicative skills in school-aged children with autism spectrum disorder.' *Adapted Physical Activity Quarterly 30*, 271–282.

Malecki, C.K. and Elliott, S.N. (2002) 'Children's social behaviors as predictors of academic achievement: A longitudinal analysis.' *School Psychology Quarterly 17*, 1–23.

March, J.S., Conners, C., Arnold, G., Epstein, J., *et al.* (1999) 'The Multidimensional Anxiety Scale for Children (MASC): Confirmatory factor analysis in a pediatric ADHD sample.' *Journal of Attention Disorders 3*, 2, 85–89.

Matson, J.L., Matson, M.L., and Rivet, T.T. (2007) Social-skills treatments for children with autism spectrum disorders: An overview.' *Behavior Modification 31*, 5, 682–707.

Maurice, C., Green, G., and Luce, S.C. (1996) *Behavioral Intervention for Young Children with Autism: A Manual for Parents and Professionals.* Austin, TX: Pro-Ed, Inc.

McGee, G.G., Almeida, M.C., Sulzer-Azaroff, B., and Feldman, R.S. (1992) 'Promoting reciprocal interactions via peer incidental teaching.' *Journal of Applied Behavior Analysis 25*, 1, 117–126.

McGee, G.G., Morrier, M.J., and Daly, T. (1999) 'An incidental teaching approach to early intervention for toddlers with autism.' *Journal of the Association for Persons with Severe Handicaps 24*, 3, 133–146.

Moore, D.W., Anderson, A., Treccase, F., Deppeler, J., Furlonger, B., and Didden, R. (2013) 'A video-based package to teach a child with autism spectrum disorder to write her name.' *Journal of Developmental and Physical Disabilities 25*, 5, 493–503.

Moore, H., Barton, E., and Chironis, M. (2014) 'A program for improving toddler communication through parent coaching.' *Topics in Early Childhood Special Education 33*, 4, 212–224.

Murphy, H.A., Hutchison, J.M., and Bailey, J.S. (1983) 'Behavioral school psychology goes outdoors: The effect of organized games on playground aggression.' *Journal of Applied Behavior Analysis 16*, 1, 29–32.

Myles, B.S., Hagan, K., Holverstott, J., Hubbard, A., Adreon, D.A., and Trautman, M. (2005) *Life Journey through Autism: An Educator's Guide to Asperger Syndrome.* Accessed on 02/04/2019 at https://researchautism.org/wp-content/uploads/2016/11/An_Educators_Guide_to_Asperger_Syndrome.pdf

Myles, B.S., Trautman, M.L., and Schelvan, R.S. (2004) *The Hidden Curriculum: Practical Solutions for Understanding Unstated Rules in Social Situations.* Shawnee Mission, KS: Autism Asperger Publishing Company.

National Research Council (2001) *Educating Children with Autism*. Committee on Educational Interventions for Children with Autism. C. Lord and J.P. McGee (eds). Washington, DC: National Academy Press, Division of Behavioral and Social Sciences and Education. Accessed on 02/04/2019 at www.nap.edu/catalog/10017/educating-children-with-autism

Nelson, C., McDonnell, A.P., Johnston, S.S., Crompton, A., and Nelson, A.R. (2007) 'Keys to play: A strategy to increase the social interactions of young children with autism and their typically developing peers.' *Education and Training in Developmental Disabilities 42*, 2, 165–181.

Odom, S.L., Brown, W.H., Frey, T., Karasu, N., Smith-Canter, L.L., and Strain, P.S. (2003) 'Evidence based practices for young children with autism: Contributions for single-subject design research.' *Focus on Autism and Other Developmental Disabilities 18*, 166–176.

Orsmond, G.I., Krauss, M.W., and Seltzer, M.M. (2004) 'Peer relationships and social and recreational activities among adolescents and adults with autism.' *Journal of Autism and Developmental Disorders 34*, 3, 245–256.

Owen-DeSchryver, J.S., Carr, E.G., Cale, S.I., and Blakeley-Smith, A. (2008) 'Promoting social interactions between students with autism spectrum disorders and their peers in inclusive school settings.' *Focus on Autism and Other Developmental Disabilities 23*, 1, 15–28.

Phelps-Terasaki, D. and Phelps-Gunn, T. (2007) *TOPL-2 Test of Pragmatic Language: Examiner's Manual*, 2nd edn. Austin, TX: Pro-Ed, Inc.

Powers, E.N. and Powers, M.D. (2000) 'For kids only: Tips for being a friend with a student with autism.' *Autism-Asperger's Digest* (July–August), 14–16.

Prizant, B.M. and Rubin, E. (1999) 'Contemporary issues in interventions for autism spectrum disorders: A commentary.' *Journal of the Association for Persons with Severe Handicaps 24*, 3, 199–208.

Quinn, M.M., Kavale, K.A., Mathur, S.R., Rutherford Jr., R.B., and Forness, S.R. (1999) 'A meta-analysis of social skills interventions for students with emotional and behavioral disorders.' *Journal of Emotional and Behavioral Disorders 7*, 54–64.

Reynolds, C.R. and Kamphaus, R.W. (1992) *BASC: Behavior Assessment System for Children*. Circle Pines, MN: American Guidance Service.

Ricks, D.M. and Wing, L. (1975) 'Language, communication and the use of symbols in normal and autistic children.' *Journal of Autism and Childhood Schizophrenia 5*, 191–221.

Rinehart, N.J., Bradshaw, J.L., Brereton, A.V., and Tonge, B.J. (2002) 'A clinical and neurobehavioural review of high-functioning autism and Asperger's disorder.' *Australian and New Zealand Journal of Psychiatry 36*, 762–770.

Rogers, S. (2000) 'Interventions that facilitate socialization in children with autism.' *Journal of Autism and Developmental Disorders 30*, 399–409.

Ross, H.S. and Kay, D.A. (1980) 'The Origins of Social Games.' In K.H. Rubin (ed.) *Children's Play*. San Francisco, CA: Jossey-Bass.

Rubin, K. (2002) *The Friendship Factor*. New York: Viking.

Rynders, J., Johnson, R., Johnson, D., and Schmidt, B. (1980) 'Effects of cooperative goal structuring in producing positive interaction between Down syndrome and nonhandicapped teenagers: Implications for mainstreaming.' *American Journal of Mental Deficiency 85*, 268–273.

Sale, P. and Carey, D.M. (1995) 'The sociometric status of students with disabilities in a full-inclusion school.' *Exceptional Children 62*, 6–19.

Schleien, S.J., Mustonen, T., and Rynders, J.E. (1995) 'Participation of children with autism and nondisabled peers in a cooperatively structured community art program.' *Journal of Autism and Developmental Disorders 25*, 4, 397–413.

Schreibman, L. (1988) *Autism*. Thousand Oaks, CA: Sage Publications, Inc.

Shtayermman, O. (2007) 'Peer victimization in adolescents and young adults diagnosed with Asperger's Syndrome: A link to depressive symptomatology, anxiety symptomatology and suicidal ideation.' *Issues in Comprehensive Pediatric Nursing 30*, 3, 87–107.

Siegel, B. (2003) *Helping Children with Autism Learn*. New York: Oxford University Press.

Sigman, M. and Ruskin, E. (1999) 'Continuity and change in the social competence of children with autism, Down syndrome, and developmental delays.' *Monographs of the Society for Research in Child Development 64*, 1–114.

Simpson, R.L., McKee, M., Teeter, D., and Beytien, A. (2007) 'Evidence-based methods for children and youth with autism spectrum disorders: Stakeholder issues and perspectives.' *Exceptionality 15*, 4, 203–217.

Siperstein, G.N., Norins, J., and Mohler, A. (2007) 'Social Acceptance and Attitude Change: Fifty Years of Research.' In J.W. Jacobson, J.A. Mulick, and J. Rojahn (eds) *Handbook of Intellectual and Developmental Disabilities*. Washington, DC: Springer.

Strain, P.S. (1991) 'Ensuring Quality of Early Intervention for Children with Severe Disabilities.' In L. Meyer, C.A. Peck, and L. Brown (eds) *Critical Issues in the Lives of People with Severe Disabilities*. Baltimore, MD: Paul H. Brookes Publishing Co.

Strain, P.S., Odom, S.L., and McConnell, S. (1984) 'Promoting social reciprocity of exceptional children: Identification, target behavior selection and intervention.' *Remedial and Special Education 5*, 1, 21–28.

Strain, P.S. and Schwartz, I. (2001) 'ABA and the development of meaningful social relations for young children with autism.' *Focus on Autism and Other Developmental Disabilities 169*, 2, 120–128.

Sugai, G., Horner, R.H., and Sprague, J. (1999) 'Functional assessment-based behavior support planning: Research-to-practice-to-research.' *Behavioral Disorders 24*, 223–227.

Tantam, D. (2000) 'Psychological disorder in adolescents and adults with Asperger syndrome.' *Autism 4*, 1, 47–62.

Taylor, B.A. (2001) 'Teaching Peer Social Skills to Children with Autism.' In C. Maurice, G. Green, and R.M. Foxx (eds) *Making A Difference*. Austin, TX: PRO-ED.

Taylor, G. (1997) 'Community building in schools: Developing a circle of friends.' *Educational and Child Psychology 14*, 45–50.

Tsao, L. and Odom, S.L. (2006) 'Sibling-mediated social interaction intervention for young children with autism.' *Topics in Early Childhood Education 26*, 2, 106–123.

Twachtman-Cullen, D. and Twachtman-Reilly, J. (2002) *How Well Does Your IEP Measure Up? Quality Indicators for Effective Service Delivery*. Higganum, CT: Starfish Specialty Press.

Vicker, B. (2009) 'Meeting the challenge of social pragmatics with students on the autism spectrum.' *The Reporter 14*, 2, 11–17.

Vygotsky, L.S. (1978) *Mind in Society: The Development of Higher Psychological Processes*. Cambridge, MA: Harvard University Press.

Wagner, S. (2002) *Inclusive Programming for Middle School Students with Autism/ Asperger's Syndrome*. Arlington, TX: Future Horizons, Inc.

Weatherby, A.M. and Prizant, B.M. (1992) 'Facilitating Language and Communication Development in Autism: Assessment and Intervention Guidelines.' In D.E. Berkell (ed.) *Autism: Identification, Education and Treatment*. Hillsdale, NJ: Lawrence Erlbaum Associates.

Werner, G.A., Vismara, L.A., Koegel, R.L., and Koegel, L.K. (2006) 'Play Dates, Social Interactions, and Friendships.' In R.L. Koegel and L.K. Koegel (eds) *Pivotal Response Treatments for Autism: Communication, Social, & Academic Development*. Baltimore, MD: Paul H. Brookes Publishing Co.

Whitaker, P., Barratt, P., Joy, H., Potter, M., and Thomas, G. (1998) 'Children with autism and peer group support: using "circle of friends".' *British Journal of Special Education 25*, 2, 60–64.

Wiig, E.H. and Secord, W. (1989) *Test of Language Competence—Expanded Edition*. New York: The Psychological Corporation.

Williams, E., Reddy, V., and Costall, A. (2001) 'Taking a closer look at functional play in children with autism.' *Journal of Autism and Developmental Disorders 31*, 1, 67–77.

Wing, L. (1981) 'Asperger's syndrome: A clinical account.' *Psychological Medicine 11*, 115–129.

Winner, M.G. (2000) *Inside Out: What Makes the Person with Social Cognitive Deficits Tick*. San Jose, CA: Think Social Publishing, Inc.

Winner, M.G. (2006) *Thinking About You, Thinking About Me*. Self-published, www.socialthinking.com, San Jose, CA.

Wolfberg, P.J. (2003) *Peer Play and the Autism Spectrum: The Art of Guiding Children's Socialization and Imagination*. Shawnee Mission, KS: Autism Asperger Publishing Company.

Wolfberg, P., DeWitt, M., Young, G.S., and Nguyen, T. (2015) 'Integrated play groups: Promoting symbolic and social engagement with typical peers in children with ASD across settings.' *Journal of Autism and Developmental Disorders*, DOI 10.1007/ s10803-014-2245-0.

Wood, J.J., Drahota, A., Sze, K., Har, K., Chiu, A., and Langer, D.A. (2009) 'Cognitive behavioral therapy for anxiety in children with autism spectrum disorders: A randomized, controlled trial.' *Journal of Child Psychology and Psychiatry 50*, 224–234.

Yuill, N., Strieth, S., Roake, C., Aspden, A., and Todd, B. (2007) 'Brief report: Designing a playground for children with autistic spectrum disorders – effects on playful peer interactions.' *Journal of Autism and Developmental Disorders 37*, 1192–1196.

Zachman, L., Huisingh, R., Barrett, M., Orman, J., *et al.* (1994) *Tasks of Problem Solving: Adolescent—Elementary Revised*. East Moline, IL: LinguiSystems, Inc.

The Contributors

Sharman Ober-Reynolds, MSN, FNP, CCRP, is Senior Research Coordinator at Southwest Autism Research & Resource Center in Phoenix, AZ. She is also the founder of the FRIEND® program, which she has been using and refining for over 18 years.

Christopher J. Smith, PhD, is the Vice President and Research Director at Southwest Autism Research & Resource Center. He has a wealth of professional experience in neurodevelopmental conditions, and ASD in particular.

Lori Vincent, PhD, BCBA-D, is a licensed psychologist in the Division of Developmental and Behavioral Pediatrics at Cincinnati Children's Hospital Medical Center. She completed her doctoral training in school psychology at the University of Wisconsin-Madison and her psychology internship and post-doctoral fellowship at the Kennedy Krieger Institute/ Johns Hopkins School of Medicine. Her clinical work and research focuses on evidence-based interventions for children with Autism Spectrum Disorder and other developmental disabilities.

Holly Sokol, MEd, originally trained as a music therapist and provided services to children and adults for six years. For the last nine years, she has worked as a special education teacher in settings ranging from self-contained classrooms to her current resource setting at Legacy Traditional Schools.

Sheri S. Dollin, MEd, is an early childhood educator with decades of experience supporting individuals with autism and promoting welcoming environments. Her collaborative partnerships include state and national projects related to disabilities, behavior, inclusion, training, and education.

Sheri played a key role at the Southwest Autism Research & Resource Center in building programs, leading innovative projects, and growing the organization's footprint. More recently, she works in the non-profit space to impact the early childhood workforce in the delivery of quality early childhood education and care. Her passion for helping others find solutions includes teaching mindfulness to parents, individuals with autism, and professionals.

Southwest Autism Research & Resource Center
300 N. 18th Street
Phoenix, Arizona 85006
Fax: 602.340.8720
Email: sarrc@autismcenter.org
www.autismcenter.org

Index

Sub-headings in *italics* indicate tables and figures.